8/19

MINERAL COUNTY LIBRARY
P.O. BOX 1390
HAWTHORNE, NV 89415

D1012124

A-Z OF GROWING UP, PUBERTY AND SEX

★ INDEX

A-Z OF GROWING UP, PUBERTY AND SEX

LESLEY DE MEZA & STEPHEN DE SILVA

W
FRANKLIN WATTS
LONDON·SYDNEY

CONTENTS

Published in paperback in 2018 by The Watts Publishing Group

Copyright © The Watts Group 2013

All rights reserved.

Editor: Paul Rockett
Design: www.rawshock.co.uk
Cover Designer: Peter Scoulding
Illustrator: Peter Lubach

Dewey number: 612.6'61
ISBN: 978 1 4451 6356 7

Every attempt has been made to clear copyright. Should there be any inadvertent omission please apply to the publisher for rectification.

Printed in Malaysia

Franklin Watts
An imprint of
Hachette Children's Group
Part of The Watts Publishing Group
Carmelite House
50 Victoria Embankment
London EC4Y 0DZ

An Hachette UK Company

www.hachette.co.uk
www.franklinwatts.co.uk

MIX
Paper from
responsible sources
FSC® C104740

❋ INTRODUCTION

This book does what it says on the cover – you'll find information about growing up, puberty and sex listed in alphabetical order. There are lots of different headings – for example, love, pregnancy, sexually transmitted infections (STIs) and so on. We asked many people what should be in this book and have tried to cover everything they suggested. We think all young people are entitled to be able to find out the information they need to have safe and happy lives.

The right information

Some adults may think some of the contents are too detailed or perhaps provide too much information for someone your age. However, when we've talked to young people like you they tell us that TV soap operas, the Internet and other media offer this information too – although they don't always provide enough detail or can at times be inaccurate. It is the intention of this book to give information in an accurate, accessible and balanced way.

Puberty happens for different people at different times – so this book is aimed at answering the kind of questions you may have as you go through this stage in your life.

Not just biology

We also found that many young people said that the sex education they had at school often focused mostly on biology. We've included several pieces which are about the emotional and 'feelings' side of growing up. We have also written about some of the decisions you may need to make as you go through puberty.

When to have sex

We know that families have different beliefs about sex; sometimes these are guided by the religion or culture that they belong to. You'll find throughout this book we've taken a particular point-of-view, not informed by religious beliefs, which is that it's better to wait until you are older to have sex. We make no apologies for this, because as you mature you will develop a better understanding of the responsibilities and consequences of starting a sexual relationship. You will have gained a better sense of yourself (who you are) and not be swayed by pressure from a partner, friends, the media etc.

Talking about it

Some people don't find it easy to talk about sex, while others don't find it a problem. There is no law against asking questions about sex – throughout the book we've said to please ask your parents, adult family members and other trusted adults if there's something you want to know about.

You can also get answers from reliable agencies – you will find a list in the back of this book. We have chosen those that specialise in working with young people and they are there to listen and offer confidential help and advice. They won't judge you.

Finding the right words

We know that different words are used to describe some of the things we've written about in this book. We have used the 'correct terminology' for our main headings but you'll also find that we've listed other words that you may have heard.

At the end of each entry, you will find a 'See also' list to guide you to other entries which may be of interest. You will also find a 'You were looking for ...' list, which will direct you to an entry that corresponds to what you may have been searching for under that letter and cannot find.

We hope you find this book useful and that you enjoy reading it.

Stephen De Silva and Lesley de Meza

ABORTION

Abortion is the termination (ending) of a pregnancy. All sorts of women all over the world use abortion services. Unintended pregnancy can occur to people in every culture, faith or religion. Abortion in the UK is legal, but there are agreed legal reasons that must be satisfied if you are to be allowed an abortion. Two doctors must sign a certificate agreeing to it.

What happens

Abortion or termination of pregnancy (TOP), as it is sometimes called, can involve one of several methods:

- Taking a series of prescribed medications that cause a miscarriage (usually up to 9 weeks pregnant);
- Under local or general anaesthetic, suctioning away the contents of the uterus (womb) through a tube (usually between 5–15 weeks pregnant);
- In later pregnancy, other abortion methods are available.

What you need to do

Whatever age you are, you are entitled to a confidential consultation with a doctor, provided you make it clear that you do not want a parent to be told. However, a doctor may refuse to discuss the matter if you are under 16. Health providers will usually prefer you to discuss an abortion with your parent(s) and will try to persuade you to do so.

You could seek help from a young person's advice centre or a local family planning centre (look in your local telephone directory).

It is important that young people who have had, or who may go on to have, an abortion do not feel cut-off, distressed or sneered at.

SEE ALSO:

ADOPTION page 11
CONFIDENTIAL page 27
CONTRACEPTION page 28
PREGNANCY page 66

ABSTAIN A

When you 'abstain' you voluntarily choose not to do something: you make a clear decision based on your beliefs or values. Some people believe that it is right for teenagers to abstain from sexual contact.

Pressure to 'do it'

Abstaining is a personal choice – a lot of people abstain for moral or religious reasons or for the fact that they simply prefer sex in a loving relationship and want to wait until then.

It will be better to abstain until you can make your own mind up – it is also important to educate yourself and check that you understand all the issues. Making an informed choice to abstain is a positive step – nobody should feel forced into abstaining because someone tells you to or tries to scare you to do so.

You may feel under pressure to have sex from others. It can be very easy to have sex because you think everyone else is and that it's the normal thing to do. It can take willpower and a strong sense of self-respect not to give in to such pressure and abstain. It's also quite often not true that 'everyone is doing it' – and even if everyone is 'doing it' it doesn't mean you have to.

SEE ALSO:

AGE OF CONSENT page 12
CELIBACY page 20
PEER PRESSURE page 61

Abuse means that a person is being mistreated, sometimes cruelly, by another person. Abuse can take several forms.

Forms of abuse
Physical abuse may involve hitting, shaking or otherwise causing physical harm.

Emotional abuse can be felt when people are being cruel/nasty and telling a person they are worthless or unloved. It may involve seeing or hearing the ill-treatment of another but not intervening, causing someone to feel frightened or in danger.

Sexual abuse involves forcing someone to take part in any kind of sexual acts that they do not choose to do for themselves. This can include forcing someone to be involved in prostitution or pornography.

Neglect means not looking after someone's basic physical and/or emotional needs. For example, not protecting a person from physical harm or danger; not providing adequate food, clothing or shelter; stopping someone having medical care or treatment.

Awareness
Awareness of abuse is usually focused on adults harming children. However, abuse also happens between young people. For example girl/boyfriend relationships where one tries to control the other is a kind of abuse. So is unnecessary jealousy or anger with another person.

   If you are being abused, or you know someone who is, help and support are available. Talk to a trusted adult at home or school or call a support number (see *Useful contacts*). They will listen and advise what to do next.

SEE ALSO:

BULLYING page 19
INTERNET SAFETY page 52
PORNOGRAPHY page 65
RAPE page 71
SEXUAL HARASSMENT page 76

YOU WERE LOOKING FOR ...

ACNE go to ZITS page 87

Adoption is when a young person legally becomes the child of someone other than their birth parent(s). For all sorts of reasons a person's birth parent(s) may be unable to care for them, temporarily. Often, if no one else in the family is able to help, foster-parents will look after the child/young person, for a while. Every so often some birth parents need to make this situation permanent.

Why does adoption happen?

Children may be given up for adoption for all sorts of reasons: sometimes birth parents are not old enough to bring up a child or they may be unable to cope or their circumstances mean they have no other choice. The word 'adoption' has several meanings, two of which are 'acceptance' and 'embrace'. Adopted children have been found and chosen at great trouble.

The law

Adopted children are treated in law as if they had been born to the person/couple who adopted them. They, not the birth parents, have full legal responsibility for the children. People who adopt are advised to be open with their adopted children and to inform them of their origins. This is obviously a very sensitive issue but it is probably better to talk about it proudly instead of hiding it.

At 18, people who have been adopted have a right to see a copy of their original birth records and to ask for more information about their birth parents from the agency which arranged their adoption.

SEE ALSO:

A ▶ AGE OF CONSENT

'Consent' means agreement. The age of consent is the age when the law says you can agree to have sex. However – it doesn't mean you have to have sex! 'Sex' means penetrative sex, oral sex or masturbating together.

In the UK the age of consent is 16 for heterosexuals, gay men and lesbians. The age varies from country to country. Until you reach this age you can't legally have sex with anyone, however old they are. It is also illegal to:

- have sex without both people giving their full consent. If someone says 'no', it means no;
- have sex with someone who is unable to give their consent. This could be because they don't understand what is happening, e.g. due to disability.

What if we're under 16 and our parents say it's okay?
That doesn't make any difference – your parents don't make the law. The age of consent law always applies.

What happens if you have underage sex?
The law sees it as sexual assault – a criminal offence. In general, the bigger the age difference between the two people having sex, the harsher the older person will be punished, especially if the older person is already over the age of consent.

Everyone is ready for sex at different ages. The law is there to protect as many people as possible, especially those who are most vulnerable, such as those under the age of 16 and people with learning difficulties.

Bereavement is the sense of loss that a person feels, especially at the death of someone they care about. The effect on each person will be different, but most people feel great pain, sorrow and a sense of loss.

When someone we care about dies we may experience all sorts of changes in how we feel emotionally and physically. Bereavement can sometimes negatively affect our friendships with others or our family relationships, especially if it seems as if others are not feeling what we are feeling.

Feelings

Bereavement can bring up all sorts of emotions, such as shock, anger, fear, guilt, relief and sadness. It is common for people to experience these over a long period of time and the same feelings can come back even when you had thought they had gone away. After some time most people find that the feelings are not so intense or are easier to deal with. One bereaved person put it like this: 'Life will never be the same. It's different. And that's OK.'

Bereavement is a natural feeling that we will all go through – but for some people it can be overwhelming. If you or someone you know needs help with their feelings of bereavement then talk to someone. Don't bottle your feelings up or feel you should just be able to cope.

Body odour (BO) describes unwanted and sometimes embarrassing smells, often from our armpits.

As you grow up your body starts to change. You can see the changes on the outside – you will probably notice that your hair and skin may be a bit greasier – but you can't always see the other changes.

The changes that occur during puberty are due to hormones. Hormones are chemical substances that prepare your body for adulthood and are the reason you will sweat more than before, particularly under your arms and around your genitals. In these areas you produce oils and proteins as well as sweat. The bacteria we have on our skin feeds off these and this often leaves a really awful smell.

Keeping clean

So you need to make sure you wash every day and not just your hands and face. Having a daily bath or shower works best, but if you can't do that remember your armpits, bottom, genitals, feet and toes – they all need a good daily wash.

It's no good just putting deodorant on in an effort to cover up smells. To work properly deodorant needs to go onto clean skin. Don't use deodorants on your genitals; they contain perfume and other ingredients which could give you a rash and upset your body's own chemical balance.

Wearing clothes made from natural fibres like cotton or wool is a good idea. It helps if you've got clean underwear and socks to wear every day too.

SEE ALSO:

PUBERTY: BOYS page 68
PUBERTY: GIRLS page 69
UNDERWEAR page 83

YOU WERE LOOKING FOR …

BLACKHEADS go to ZITS
page 87
BLOW JOB go to ORAL SEX
page 58

BODY IMAGE B

'Body image' is the way we see our body or how we think others see us.

Body shapes and fashions have changed throughout history. Rounder and more filled out was popular in the past but nowadays being skinny is 'in'… unless of course you are skinny then you usually want to be curvier or more muscly!

Perfection?
We are surrounded by images of perfection every day: on TV, in magazines and in advertising. If you don't have the perfect body (and most of us don't!) these images may leave you feeling … well, 'lacking'.

Many images you see, whether printed in a magazine, or filmed, have been air-brushed (changed with computer programmes) to make them appear perfect. If you don't like your body and it seems that many of us don't, this can have a really depressing effect on our well-being and self-esteem.

Happy?
Being happy doesn't depend on how we look on the outside, it's also about appreciating the person that exists on the inside. If you were choosing a best friend you wouldn't just go by what they looked like. You would probably want a friend who is caring, fun, honest, humorous, loyal and trustworthy. In other words, when you look under the surface you find what really matters.

Braces are a piece of equipment used by orthodontists to correct the position of teeth. Orthodontics is a Greek word that literally means 'to straighten teeth'.

There are many types of braces and your orthodontist will advise which will work best for you. Metal braces are still used, but you might be able to get clear braces or braces that are the same colour as your teeth. There are even braces that go behind your teeth where no one can see them.

Food can easily get stuck in your braces, so you need to keep your teeth especially clean. It will help to brush after meals and be extra careful to get out any food that gets stuck.

Braces put pressure on your teeth so you might feel uncomfortable once in a while, especially after the orthodontist makes adjustments.

Why braces?

Braces can make us feel self-conscious but they're temporary and it's worth thinking about the future difference they'll make – be they for medical or cosmetic reasons. Having a great smile of your own can help you build self-confidence and feel good about yourself. However, lots of people don't have perfect teeth, so don't worry if yours aren't straight. Take a look at most of your friends or people you know. Many of them probably don't have straight teeth either. Sometimes teeth just don't grow evenly.

SEE ALSO:

BODY IMAGE page 15
CONFIDENCE page 26

YOU WERE LOOKING FOR …

BRAINS go to EXAMS page 39

Simply put, a bra is a piece of underwear designed to support and shape a woman's breasts. A bra can be made of all different types of materials: cotton, lace, nylon, satin... even leather or rubber. The list is endless!

Some girls start growing breasts when they're in primary school and others don't until they're in secondary. Don't worry about this – we are all different! Some girls get really excited at the prospect of having their first bra and others loathe the idea; whatever age or stage of development you are at, the choice of whether or not to wear a bra is a personal one. Generally, most women find it more comfortable to wear one than not.

Support and fittings

Whether large or small, breasts need to be properly supported. Breasts don't contain muscles – they are made up of delicate glandular tissue.

A well fitted bra is really important to avoid back pain and sore shoulders (from badly fitting or positioned straps). A well-fitted bra can also help to improve posture, overall appearance and enhance self-esteem. It will also play an important part in how your clothes fit and look on your body.

If you decide you want to wear a bra, ask for help from your mother, another female relative or you could approach an underwear specialist in a shop.

SEE ALSO:

BREASTS

Breasts are the two globes of flesh on a woman's chest. They are also known as: boobs, bosoms, jugs, melons or tits.

Until you go through puberty you will just have nipples, not breasts. When puberty starts you'll probably notice that you develop little lumps behind your nipples – these are known as breast buds and they will eventually begin to grow into breasts. Breasts continue to develop until you're about 20 by which time they will have more or less evened out.

As your breasts grow, your nipples will get bigger and may darken in colour. You might notice a feeling of discomfort in your breasts and/or some tingling. They will become very sensitive – and if you get accidentally knocked in the breast it can be painful as they are very tender. Breasts may feel sore in the week before your period – that's quite normal. Breasts and nipples can also give us pleasure when they are touched; that's because they contain lots of sensitive nerve endings.

Size doesn't matter!
Breasts come in a variety of shapes and sizes. Most of us will have one breast slightly bigger than the other – it's usually not noticeable. Whether you've got big bosoms or little breasts it doesn't matter: all are feminine and attractive. Remember, it's not true that people prefer girls/women with large breasts. Everyone has different preferences.

One of the main reasons we have breasts is to enable us to breastfeed babies: breasts contain glands that produce milk. The size of breasts makes no difference to breastfeeding.

SEE ALSO:

BODY IMAGE page 15
BRA page 17
PERIODS page 62
PUBERTY: GIRLS page 69

A bully tries to hurt others physically or by making them feel uncomfortable, calling them names or spreading rumours about them. The bully may hurt the other person repeatedly. Bullying can happen to anyone at any age and can happen at school, at home or online.

Bullying can be:
- **About class or background** – for example, calling somebody a 'chav' or 'snob';
- **Disabilist** – harming others or using offensive language to describe people who are disabled;
- **Homophobic** – using words like 'gay' as an insult;
- **About the way someone looks** – e.g. having ginger hair, wearing glasses, being overweight;
- **Racist** – using offensive words or actions because of someone's race, the colour of their skin, where they are from or what they believe.

If someone is bullying you
Tell someone you trust about being bullied. If it is easier, write that person a note instead – talk to parents, teachers or older friends. If they do not do anything, find someone else. Never keep being bullied a secret.

If you see someone who is being bullied
Get friends together and talk to the bully – let them know that bullying is not acceptable and you won't stand by. If it doesn't stop then find someone to help stop it. Be friendly and get to know the people who are being bullied. Try to make friends with the bully too – show them that there are better ways to interact with others.

Being celibate originally described someone who made a religious vow not to get married. This came from a belief that having a married relationship would distract them from their main purpose in focusing on God and serving others. Today 'celibacy' is often used more widely to describe anyone who chooses not to have a sexual relationship for all or part of their life.

It can be hard for someone who is celibate to explain this choice. The world around us focuses very strongly on the idea that having a loving, sexual relationship with another individual is the best way to live. So choosing to be celibate can result in others being baffled by your choice and poking fun at you.

Why celibacy?
In addition to the religious viewpoint, people who are celibate give other reasons for making this life-choice.

- **Self-esteem** – they feel that they do not need to have a sexual relationship to make them feel important or valued.
- **Time** – some people feel the pressures of a career or other commitments in their life do not leave them sufficient time to have an intimate relationship. They may feel that they are being fairer to others by not trying to have a relationship when they cannot give the other person the time and attention they deserve.
- **Personal strength** – when someone makes a conscious choice to do or not do something, it can give a sense of control and purpose in their lives.

The phrase 'chatting up' describes when one person shows a romantic or sexual interest in another. They start a conversation so that they get to know them better and perhaps even ask them out.

If you decide to chat somebody up it might be helpful to remember a few basic guidelines.

- **Don't brag too much or invent things about yourself** – they are likely to find out the truth eventually!
- **Show interest in the other person not just for their looks** – take some time to find out what they like, their interests, what sort of personality they have.
- **Let them know a few things about yourself** – your interests, hobbies etc. In the same way you are finding out stuff about them, they are finding out about you too.

Don't assume that because someone is interested in you they necessarily want to be your boy/girlfriend – they may just really like you.

If you do start getting the feeling that they really aren't interested in you as a boy/girlfriend then don't push it and make yourself unwelcome. They may turn out to be a really good friend – and we all value those. If it feels like they are interested in you too, then go for it – ask them out on a date.

C ▸ CIRCUMCISION

All boys are born with a fold of skin covering all or part of the end of their penis – this is called the foreskin and the end of the penis is called the glans. Circumcision is the removal of the foreskin and this usually happens at an early age.

UNCIRCUMCISED

Circumcision can be part of a religious or cultural tradition. For example, Jewish and Muslim boys will be circumcised as a sign of their membership to their faith. Other parents have their sons circumcised because they consider it is easier to keep the penis clean that way – so they believe it is healthier to do so. Occasionally doctors will suggest that a boy born with a very tight foreskin that cannot roll back over the glans of the penis should be circumcised – this may make sex more comfortable for them in the future.

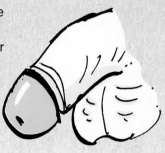

CIRCUMCISED

Attitudes to circumcision
People often feel very strongly about whether a boy should be circumcised or not. Those for circumcision argue it is more hygienic, those against circumcision argue it reduces the sensitivity of the penis. Whether a boy is circumcised or not has no effect on his ability to have sex.

'Female circumcision' is a phrase inaccurately used to describe what is more commonly known as female genital mutilation – when some or all parts of a girl's external genitals are removed.

SEE ALSO:
GENITALS: MALE page 48

Cold sores are inflamed blisters that appear most commonly around the mouth and they often start with a tingling, itching or burning sensation. Small fluid-filled blisters will then appear, usually on the edges of your lower lip. They are caused by a herpes virus (HSV-1) and usually clear up without treatment within 7–10 days.

The 'cold sore virus' is highly contagious and can be easily passed from one person to another by close personal contact. Cold sores are different to the strand of herpes virus that causes genital herpes (HSV-2). However, cold sores can be transferred to the genitals through oral sex in the same way that genital herpes can be transferred to the mouth.

Once a person has got the cold sore virus, it remains inactive for most of the time. However, certain things can trigger an outbreak, such as being really low on energy or in some women, the start of their period.

Some people get cold sores a few times a year, others have one cold sore and never have another and some never get cold sores at all because the virus never becomes active.

Prevention

If you are susceptible to cold sores there are some things you can do to help prevent a recurrence:

- Avoid direct contact with the sores on every part of the body;
- Wash your hands after touching the lips;
- Avoid picking at the sores as this can spread the virus;
- Strengthen your body's defences by leading a healthy lifestyle: eat a varied diet, exercise regularly and get enough sleep;
- Exposure to the sun can cause an outbreak. Using a sun block may help to prevent this.

Identifying yourself as lesbian or gay and then telling other people about this is often referred to as 'coming out'.

Positive effects

The first part is a gradual experience as a person starts to realise that their affections and interests lie in people of their own gender. Many friends and relatives will assume the gay/lesbian person is straight (heterosexual) so they reach a stage when they want to come out to those around them. Lots of people find that coming out is a positive experience. They are happier not having to keep a part of themselves 'hidden'.

Negative effects

Depending on the people around you, it can also have negative effects on social relationships, school or work, and self-esteem. Not surprisingly many people fear being shunned by or upsetting the people they are close to. In many parts of the world strong cultural/religious attitudes and discriminatory laws make coming out even harder.

Being open

If you think you might be gay it is probably better to take time and talk to one or two trusted people first who can help you understand the issues and decide when and how to tell others.

Lots of individuals have been more willing in recent years to talk openly about being gay or lesbian. Television soap operas, dramas, media and music programmes have featured characters and performers who speak openly about being gay/lesbian.

Condoms are sheaths worn over the penis. They are used both as a contraceptive and to protect against cervical cancer and sexually transmitted infections (STIs) including HIV/AIDS. If used properly, a condom is 98% effective at preventing pregnancy. They are also known as: rubbers, johnnies, French letters or love gloves.

Condoms are made of very fine latex or other stretchy materials. They fit over the erect penis to stop semen entering the other person. Condoms are tested by manufacturers in the UK and the European Union and must have CE markings to show they meet European standards. It is important to check the 'use by' date on the foil packets that contain condoms.

Using a condom correctly

When used correctly the small reservoir at the end of the condom will contain the sperm and seminal fluid after the man has ejaculated. If they are used incorrectly they can sometimes slip or split. Remember, 'properly' includes:

- Making sure that you squeeze the top of the closed end to get rid of any trapped air;
- Putting it on before starting to have sex;
- Using a new condom every time you have sex.

Where to get condoms

Condoms can be obtained free of charge from family planning/sexual health and young people's clinics, and can be bought in shops. There are also female condoms, which are made of polyurethane and have to be put inside the vagina. They are not widely available and are not as effective as male condoms.

SEE ALSO:

CONTRACEPTION page 28
EJACULATION page 36
FOREPLAY page 43
GENITALS: MALE page 48
SEX page 75

SEXUALLY TRANSMITTED
INFECTIONS page 78

Feeling confident means feeling self-assured and self-reliant; you are ready to face all the different things that can happen in life.

Your confidence during puberty

Puberty can give you extreme moods that leave you feeling not very confident, or you might be self-conscious about your changing body. Both of these reactions are normal.

We also don't feel confident when we have trouble explaining our feelings or points-of-view – people going through puberty sometimes say it's as if no-one understands them. Knowing what we believe and expressing ourselves clearly are just two ways we show our confidence and maturity – it's a sign that we're growing up.

Building your confidence

- Enjoy being yourself but also take time to find out what others think and feel.
- Boost yourself if you feel down by reflecting on your good qualities.
- Practise the skill of putting yourself into another person's shoes. This will help you develop empathy – an understanding that not everyone sees the world in the same way. This will help you be confident and at the same time respect other people's right to hold a different point-of-view.
- Help express yourself more confidently by reading news and information that is presented from several points of view. Use this to help you discuss and debate things with others.

SEE ALSO:

Keeping something confidential means keeping it private between two or more people. Everyone has confidential information about themselves that they do not want widely shared.

If I'm under 16, can I get confidential advice?

Health workers have a duty NOT to give out information about you without your consent, whatever your age, except in exceptional circumstances. If you are under 16 you are entitled to confidential consultations. Your doctor can refuse to discuss the matter if they are unwilling to accept your request for confidentiality.

Will a doctor tell anyone else – such as my parents?

Discussions with your doctor, treatments or test results stay confidential. Receptionists or anyone working there must not pass the information on, even if you are under 16. The only reason they might is to protect you or someone else from serious harm. This is unusual, and they should always try to discuss it with you first.

What about teachers and confidentiality?

Teachers cannot guarantee you total confidentiality. They might feel that you are at risk of harm. If so, they have to talk to the person in school with responsibility for child protection. You should be informed if this is taking place.

Sexual intercourse is the way women become pregnant. It is often called 'making love'. It's a pleasurable feeling so men and women may want to have intercourse but don't always want to have a baby. To prevent pregnancy people use contraception. Contraception involves personal choice and what's right for you within your religion/culture.

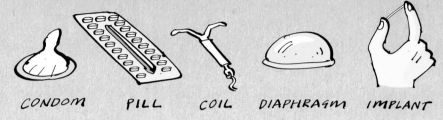

CONDOM   PILL   COIL   DIAPHRAGM   IMPLANT

Types of contraception

There are lots of different sorts of contraceptives and they work in all sorts of different ways. It's really important that people get individual advice and support to find out which method is best for them. Contraceptives include:
• cap with spermicide • combined pill • contraceptive implant
• contraceptive injection • contraceptive patch • diaphragm with spermicide • condoms (male and female) • intrauterine device (IUD or 'coil') • intrauterine system (IUS or 'mirena') • vaginal ring (nuvaring)
• sterilisation • progestogen-only pill (mini pill).

When contraception fails

If a contraceptive method fails, e.g. a condom splits or 'the pill' is forgotten, emergency contraception can be used to help prevent an unwanted pregnancy. People sometimes call emergency contraception the 'morning after pill' but that's not accurate. Emergency contraception can be used up to five days after sex, but it's more effective the sooner you take it.

You can get contraception information, advice, support and supplies (free of charge) from family planning/sexual health and young people's clinics.

SEE ALSO:
AGE OF CONSENT page 12
CONDOMS page 25
FOREPLAY page 43
SEX page 75
SEXUALLY TRANSMITTED
INFECTIONS page 78

YOU WERE LOOKING FOR …
CONSENT go to AGE OF CONSENT page 12

When you really, truly, madly deeply like one particular person –
it's usually known as having a 'crush' on them. Crushes can be
a wonderful feeling and a scary one. When you see that special
person your heart may start to race, you become nervous and
uneasy and you want their attention. If you are shy you might try
and avoid them. Sometimes, it's hard to stop thinking about them.

Crushes can be painful: you really like the person but you may
not know if he or she feels the same way – and maybe they
don't. Maybe your best friend is really good friends with
your crush and that makes you jealous. Maybe you
want to know if he or she has the
same feelings for you or if they
like someone else but you
don't want to say anything
because you feel you might
jinx it.

What love feels like

Whatever it is you're feeling
when you have a crush on
someone, don't worry it is not
unusual. Awful as it is to hear it, you
are going through a phase; you will
get over it. Then again, how can you
be sure this feeling isn't 'love'? Well,
love is a feeling that grows once you
get to know someone, whereas a crush can
happen even when you don't.

29

Cystitis is an inflammation and/or infection of the bladder. It happens mostly to women but men can also get it.

Signs of cystitis
- A stinging sensation when you wee;
- A constant urge to wee – so strong that you feel you might even wet yourself… and then when you do wee it's only a few drops;
- Your urine may be a darker colour than usual – there may even be traces of blood in it;
- You might feel quite weak, with a bit of a fever and generally feel unwell.

What to do if you have cystitis

If you do get cystitis it's a good idea to drink lots of water as this will help flush the infection out. (Cranberry juice is a good alternative to water, but avoid drinking other fruit juices as they can be very acidic.) Drink about half a pint (250ml) of water straight away and then every twenty minutes – for the next three hours.

Go to the toilet as much as you need to – don't hold on. If your school has a policy of not allowing you to go to the toilet in lesson time tell the teacher you are unwell and go straight to the school nurse or other medical staff.

You should get treatment for the infection as soon as possible to prevent the infection spreading up through your bladder and into your kidneys. If it's the first time you've had cystitis it is important that you see your doctor who will make sure the diagnosis is correct.

SEE ALSO:
DISCHARGE page 32
SEXUALLY TRANSMITTED
INFECTIONS page 78
UNDERWEAR page 83

YOU WERE LOOKING FOR …
CYBERBULLYING go to INTERNET
SAFETY page 52

Depression occurs when sad feelings do not go away and overwhelm a person, stopping them from doing the things they normally do.

Dealing with our different emotions is a normal part of our lives. Everyone finds themselves feeling happy or sad at different times. Feeling sad is usually a natural response to something worrying that is happening in our lives. These feelings usually disappear on their own when our situation improves.

Teenagers are often described as moody and withdrawn, not wanting to talk about what is bothering them. That doesn't necessarily mean they are depressed – it's probably just a normal part of adolescence.

Causes of depression

Some of the things that can cause young people to become depressed include:
- Changing school or moving home;
- Parents arguing, divorce or separation;
- Feeling rejected or left out;
- Friendship problems;
- Physical illness in themselves or in a family member;
- Poverty or homelessness;
- Problems with school work or exam pressure;
- The death of someone close to them.

If too many worries or too much is changing at once then sometimes we can feel stuck and find all this just too much to cope with. An added problem can be that if we won't talk about what is bugging us then no one knows how to help. Starting to talk is the key to dealing with depression, see *Useful contacts* at the back of the book for services that can help.

SEE ALSO:

BEREAVEMENT page 13
DIVORCE page 33
EMOTIONAL GOOD HEALTH
page 37
STRESS page 80

YOU WERE LOOKING FOR …

DATING go to CHATTING UP
page 21
DEATH go to BEREAVEMENT
page 13
DEODORANT go to BO page 14

Discharge, in biological terms, means the release of pus or liquid from the body.

Girls Having a small clear or milky discharge from the vagina is quite normal. When it dries it might be a pale yellow colour. Just before your period begins you may have more discharge that could be brownish in colour. Your discharge is there for a reason – to keep the vagina moist and healthy.

   If the discharge gets a bit smelly, itchy or turns thick or a strange colour you should go and see your doctor, or visit a sexual health/young people's clinic. You might be allergic to something or have an infection. Whatever it is, a medical professional will find out and help clear it up with prescribed treatment.

Boys
Having a discharge from the tip of the penis that is not urine or semen is not normal. It is usually a sign that something is wrong, perhaps an infection or allergic reaction. There may be other symptoms as well:
- Burning feeling when you wee;
- Frequent need to wee;
- Excessive need to wee at night (when normally you don't need to);
- A rash in the genital area, which can be painful or itchy;
- A bruised feeling in the groin.

   Whether the discharge is very little or a lot and whatever the colour, from clear to yellow or green, it requires prompt and accurate diagnosis and treatment, usually by your doctor, or visit a sexual health/young people's clinic.

SEE ALSO:
COLD SORES page 23
CYSTITIS page 30
GENITALS: FEMALE page 46
GENITALS: MALE page 48
SEXUALLY TRANSMITTED
INFECTIONS page 78

YOU WERE LOOKING FOR ...
DIAPHRAGM go to
CONTRACEPTION page 28
DICK go to GENITALS: MALE
page 48
DIET/DIETING go to
NUTRITION page 57

Divorce is when two people end their marriage or civil partnership.

When parents divorce or separate it can feel like a huge turning point in someone's life. When it happens to your parents, you can feel very alone and unsure. It may seem hard, but it is possible to cope with divorce and have a good family life in spite of the changes it brings.

Reasons for divorce

Parents divorce for many reasons. Usually it happens when couples feel they can no longer live together because the love they had when they married has changed or because one parent falls in love with someone else. It may be caused by the effect a serious problem like drinking, abuse or gambling has on the family. Sometimes nothing particularly bad happens but parents just decide to live apart.

How divorce affects you

Young people may wish they had prevented arguments between their parents by cooperating more, being better behaved or doing better at school. Children and young people need to remember that separation and divorce are a result of parents' problems with each other, and are not the children's fault.

When parents are divorcing, typical feelings may include being stressed-out, angry, frustrated or sad. Young people can end up feeling protective of one parent or blaming the other one. Others may also feel relieved, especially if there has been a lot of tension or fighting at home. These feelings are very typical and talking about them with a friend, family member or trusted adult can really help.

DUMPING AND GETTING DUMPED

There are all sorts of words that people use to describe how a relationship ends. You can: give someone the elbow, chuck a person, break up with them or dump them.

Dumping

Whichever word we use, nothing makes it very easy. If you have been seeing someone for a while but decide you want to finish it, don't be unkind in the way you do it. Honest and face-to-face is best – no one likes their relationship being ended by text, Facebook or any other means. And don't get a friend to do it for you!

Find a place to meet which each of you can easily leave if things go badly. Be honest about why you want to end things. It's okay to say, 'We've had a great time together but now I don't feel the same,' – that way no one is blamed.

Getting dumped

If you are on the receiving end, try not to get tearful or shouty. You'll probably feel really rotten and need some support from others. Tell your parents or someone else what has happened – they have probably been in that position in the past so they'll understand how you are feeling.

You might feel sad – perhaps angry and bitter too. That's okay but don't act on those negative feelings. This is a part of life and growing up. It's good to go out with lots of different people – you'll begin to get a clearer picture of who is right for you.

SEE ALSO:

CHATTING UP page 21
FANCYING page 41
RELATIONSHIPS page 72

A person is described as having an eating disorder when they begin to have problems in their relationship with food.

The three disorders you most need to be aware of are:
- **Anorexia** – an obsessive desire to lose weight or stay thin by not eating;
- **Bulimia** – eating a large quantity of food and then inducing vomiting or using large numbers of laxatives to get rid of it;
- **Binge (or compulsive) eating** – is bulimia without the purging and vomiting – which results in rapid weight gain.

People seem to develop these disorders when they have deep emotional issues, combined with low self-esteem and a feeling they lack control in an area of their life. People can be very secretive about these disorders. They affect boys and girls from all social classes and ethnic groups.

It can be very difficult to recognise when you have an eating disorder as you often try and tell yourself that nothing is wrong. For example, someone with anorexia may not think of themselves as very thin – it's as if the disorder means you can't really see yourself clearly. If you are beginning to realise that your eating patterns are going wrong then first talk with a trusted friend and see if you can go together to get some help.

What can I do to help someone with an eating disorder?
You can't fix their problems – just be there for them and listen to how they feel. Do not criticise, praise or judge their weight: encourage them to talk and to not obsess about food, calories, exercise or diets.

Eating disorders may become life-threatening. The sooner your friend gets some professional help, the sooner he/she will recover. So do not promise to keep the problem confidential. You may want to speak to someone like a school nurse or counsellor. They will help you with how you feel about seeing your friend like this. You might then want to see if your friend will see them too.

SEE ALSO:

Ejaculation describes the moment when semen comes out of the tip of a boy's penis. It may also be known as: cumming, shooting your load, shooting your wad, spunking-up or jizzing.

Semen is the liquid which carries sperm. Sperm is made in the testicles. If a boy is having intercourse or masturbating, his penis grows stiff and his body tenses. When he reaches a peak of excitement and can't hold back any longer ejaculation happens. Sperm rushes through his penis and spurts out in several spasms. It is a very pleasurable and exciting feeling.

If a male is having vaginal intercourse with a woman then his semen will be inside her body; if a male sperm and a female egg meet then fertilisation happens (the female is pregnant) and a foetus develops.

Erections

A boy almost always has an erection when he ejaculates – that means his penis has grown stiff with excitement. As soon as he ejaculates his penis will go soft again.

Most boys start to ejaculate around the age of 12 but some ejaculate before and others after that age – it depends when puberty happens and hormones cause his body to mature. Sometimes this first ejaculation takes place unexpectedly whilst he sleeps so he wakes up to a sticky mess, not realising it has happened. This is called a 'wet dream'.

Emotional health describes having balance in our feelings – but these feeling won't always stay the same. Sometimes you are feeling on top of the world and at other times down in the dumps – that's normal. It may also have a lot to do with the hormones rushing round your body as you go through puberty… and we certainly can't control them.

Look after yourself

If something happens that brings you down you feel low emotionally. It may feel as if nobody understands you; as if you're the only one who gets so much hassle; that adults really don't get it; and that the people who care for you are like aliens from another universe. Try taking some deep breaths; have something you fancy to eat and drink; chill and relax with some music, then tell yourself that this is normal and things will improve.

If you're feeling down, fed-up or depressed you will probably feel better if you talk to someone. Keeping things 'bottled-up' isn't good for anyone. There are all sorts of people you can talk to – probably it's best to start with people in your family like parents, older brothers and sisters or grandparents. If you feel you can't talk things over with someone in your family or an adult in your life, there are organisations you can contact in confidence (see *Useful contacts*).

SEE ALSO:

BEREAVEMENT page 13
BODY IMAGE page 15
CONFIDENCE page 26
DEPRESSION page 31
EATING DISORDERS page 35
STRESS page 80

YOU WERE LOOKING FOR …

EMERGENCY CONTRACEPTION go to CONTRACEPTION page 28
EMOTIONAL ABUSE go to ABUSE page 10

ERECTION

An erection describes what happens when the penis goes from being soft to stiff and firm. It is also known as: a hard-on, a stiffy, a boner, getting wood or getting the horn.

The mechanics

Inside the penis is soft, spongy tissue with lots of blood vessels running through it. Normally, blood flows in and out of the penis at a steady rate. When a male gets sexually excited a ring of muscle at the base of the penis tightens – blood flows in but can't flow out again causing the penis to stiffen and grow in size. This is an erection. When his sexual excitement dies down, for example after ejaculation, then the ring of muscle relaxes and it returns to its usual soft state.

A few males might have five or six erections and/or ejaculations while sleeping, but many others will have only one or two.

Erections vary – some penises point upwards, others will be more horizontal. Very occasionally a male might have problems with erections or ejaculations – if so, talk to a doctor.

Spontaneous erections

Boys sometimes worry about spontaneous erections – they are common during puberty and you can't stop them happening. Try making it less noticeable by sitting down or covering it with something (e.g. a book, or by tying a sweatshirt round your waist). Think about something else until it goes away. You may be embarrassed, but remember that it happens to all boys.

SEE ALSO:

EJACULATION page 36
GENITALS: MALE page 48
PUBERTY: BOYS page 68
WET DREAMS page 85

Taking examinations is a fact of life, but that doesn't make it less stressful. Some people breeze through them, keeping calm, happy and unfazed, whilst others feel physically ill, can't sleep and suffer very badly. Remind yourself and your family that you will do your best – no one can do more than that.

Revision tips

Planning in advance should enable you to deal with what you're facing and that will help put your mind at ease. Make sure you know what you'll be examined on. If you've missed any work – catch up. Ensure your notes are current and complete.

Make a revision timetable that's practical and adaptable. You may find it helpful to link it to your exam timetable, studying subjects in the right order. It's really important to give yourself time for meals, sleep, chores or other commitments, as well as time for relaxing. No one should study non-stop – you need a healthy balance.

You won't always find the peace, quiet and space to revise at home so, think about using facilities at school or your local library. If you decide to study at home, put your notes away when you aren't using them, so they're not always in your face.

There are many good revision aids available including revision guides, TV revision programmes and Internet sites. Your teachers should be able to suggest some ideas and resources to help you.

SEE ALSO:

CONFIDENCE page 26
STRESS page 80

YOU WERE LOOKING FOR ...

EXERCISE go to FITNESS
page 42

FAMILIES

We usually think of families as a group made up of parents and children. All families are different and no family is perfect.

There are all sorts of things that can help make family life easier. It's a question of give and take. Even when family life is difficult, parents have the right to expect you to behave yourself, do your homework and your jobs around the house. You have the right to expect love and support from the family around you.

Feelings

Going through adolescence takes your feelings all over the place – one minute you think your parents don't understand you, the next they embarrass you. It might feel like everyone else's parents offer fewer restrictions than yours. If a family issue gets too much to cope with, try writing down the main points and then ask if you can all sit down and talk about it. This is far more helpful than getting in a strop and slamming the bedroom door. Believe it or not, your parents were adolescents themselves, once.

Telling the truth

Sometimes young people feel so worried about something that's happened that they lie to their parents. This will make the situation worse, particularly when your parents find out, as undoubtedly they will. Telling the truth may not be easy – but parents will respect you for it and you won't risk losing their trust in you.

SEE ALSO:	YOU WERE LOOKING FOR ...
ADOPTION page 11	**FAMILY PLANNING go to**
DIVORCE page 33	**CONTRACEPTION page 28**
RELATIONSHIPS page 72	
STRESS page 80	

FANCYING: DOES HE/SHE FANCY YOU? F

L. GAGA 4 J. BIEBER

When we fancy someone it means that we are attracted to them, physically or by their personality. We don't have much say over who it is we fancy – in fact, sometimes we can fancy more than one person at a time – it just happens.

If the person you fancy spends time looking at you or catching your eye, maybe they give you a shy smile or blush when you look at them, or finds reasons to be around you – then chances are they fancy you too! You might decide you want to move things forward – sooner or later you're going to have to let them know how you feel. Choose your words carefully. 'I really fancy you' might be the most straightforward way of telling them, but it's not very romantic and might make you look silly.

Beginning

Start by paying them a few compliments about the way they look or the clothes they wear or something they do. If they haven't run away by this point then things are looking up. So it might be a good idea to ask them if they'd like to meet up with you sometime. You'll need to have thought beforehand where that might be.

If they decide they don't want to meet up with you then you'll know they don't feel the same. Don't ask them again or nag them. You haven't lost anything by asking them. You just need to accept that we don't always feel the same way about each other.

SEE ALSO:

CHATTING UP page 21
CRUSH page 29
DUMPING page 34

YOU WERE LOOKING FOR ...

FANNY go to GENITALS: FEMALE page 46
FAT go to BODY IMAGE page 15 and EATING DISORDERS page 35
FELLATIO go to ORAL SEX page 58

There are different ways of thinking about fitness – one way is to see it as a person's overall ability to live, act and think in a healthy way – keeping body, mind and spirit in good shape.

A person with a fit body is likely to be someone who eats a balanced diet and makes sure they get regular exercise. The best guideline is about 30 minutes of activity (e.g. swimming, running, walking, rollerblading) about five times a week. A fit person will be focused on more than just looking good – they will be aware that misusing some substances such as tobacco and alcohol can cause health problems, both now and later in their lives.

Fit body/fit mind

You can help keep fit mentally by keeping a good balance between working hard and socialising. Lots of people find that having an interest or hobby or belonging to a social/activity-based club gives them plenty of interest in their lives. Make sure you have time to relax and don't forget a good night's sleep. Being able to talk about what is worrying you is important – keeping things bottled up and letting worries take over can affect us physically and mentally.

SEE ALSO:

BODY IMAGE page 15
EMOTIONAL GOOD HEALTH
page 37
NUTRITION page 57

Foreplay usually refers to what people do with each other before having sexual intercourse.

Different strokes for different folks

Different people like doing different things. For some people foreplay may mean cuddling, stroking, touching and kissing one another on different places all over the body.

Foreplay is a time to use your imagination. There are so many things that can be done that don't even involve touching. Some people may dress up for each other – whilst others undress (strip).

Couples often decide to give each other a massage – using creams or massage oils; though it is really important to remember NEVER to use any sort of oils if you are going to use condoms. Oils affect the latex of condoms and make them so fragile that they get tiny holes in them, or split.

Before you begin…

Before you begin foreplay you need to think about the fact that you might get really sexually excited. When you're excited, you might get carried away and want to have sexual intercourse… and if that happens you're going to need to have thought about contraception first. Phew! Quite a lot of thinking and planning needed isn't there? Remember, the law says 16 is the age at which a person can have sex. Never feel pressured into doing anything you don't want to.

It may sound obvious – but a person who has good friends is usually someone who is a good friend to others. You will have lots of good qualities to make you a friend: you might be loyal, encouraging to others, trustworthy, interesting to talk to or a good listener. Friendship needs to be worked on.

Friends don't always have to agree with each other about absolutely everything. Most people find it's good to have friends who have similar hobbies or points of view, but who can also teach us new things or help us see something in a different way.

Different types of friendship

People have different levels of friendship. There may be a few people who are close friends. We may also have a 'wider circle of friends'. Some friends we know really well, and others we like to be around but perhaps don't see too often.

Disagreements

A real test of friendship is how two people overcome problems when they have a disagreement. Being ready to ask the other person questions to understand what went wrong is important; don't just argue, shout or walk away. Try talking about your feelings and make sure you listen to how the other person is feeling. You might find a way to stay friends – and if you don't, then at least you have tried your best and not just thrown a good friendship away on a misunderstanding.

SEE ALSO:
BULLYING page 19
PEER PRESSURE page 61
RELATIONSHIPS page 72

YOU WERE LOOKING FOR …
FRENCH KISSING go to KISSING page 54
FRENCH LETTERS go to CONDOMS page 25
FUCKING go to SEX page 75

A person who is gay is someone who feels attracted to and wants to have a sexual relationship with someone of the same sex as themselves. Men who are attracted to men are described as being 'gay' and women who are attracted to women are described as being 'lesbian'. People have felt like this throughout history and at different times and places gays/lesbians have been celebrated or persecuted, or just not spoken about.

Gay or not?

Many people feel attracted to someone of the same sex as themselves, and they wonder if this means that they are gay/lesbian. Some go on to have gay relationships whilst others find that these feelings change over time.

Using the word 'gay'

'Gay' is a description of a relationship. Some people use 'gay' as a put-down. One teenager said, 'I don't mind so much what people call me as what they mean by it… mostly with people who are seriously prejudiced it's about how they say it – they say *gay* like it's a curse, not something to be proud of.'

How many people are gay or lesbian?

This is a very difficult question to answer – it depends on whether you consider being gay/lesbian to be about feelings, actions or both. In many places it can be dangerous to be honest about being gay/lesbian – so there are probably very few reliable statistics. All the evidence points to three or four million gay and lesbian people in Britain and there are therefore going to be many millions across the whole world.

GENITALS: FEMALE

The genitals are the external parts of our bodies that include our sexual organs. A female's genitals are the sexual parts of her body between her legs, made up of:

Clitoris

Also known as: clit, button or bud.
This is a small pea-sized bump, usually covered by a small hood of flesh. It is found inside a woman's labia. It may be tiny but it has many nerve endings and gives pleasurable sexual feelings when rubbed, which can lead to an orgasm.

Labia

Also known as: lips or flaps.
The inner and outer labia are fleshy, lip-shaped folds of skin. They usually completely cover the clitoris, urethra and vagina. They are there to protect these delicate parts of the body. Labia come in many different sizes, shapes and colours.

Urethra

Also known as: wee or pee hole.
This is the tube that connects the bladder to the genitals – allowing urine to be removed from the body.

Vagina

Also known as: pussy, fanny, beaver, growler or muff.
This is the opening passage inside the labia. It leads up to the cervix and womb (uterus). It has three main functions:
- Blood from your period, leaves your body by travelling down it;
- It is the passage through which you may have sexual intercourse;
- It is the passage which stretches large enough to allow a baby to be born.

Vulva

Also known as: fairy, nunnie, lady garden, minge or cunt.
The triangular mound of fatty tissue that covers the pubic bone together with the rest of the external female genitals (clitoris, labia, urethra and vagina) are collectively known as the vulva.

Womb

Also known as the uterus.

This isn't actually part of the genitals, but as it is the organ just above the cervix at the top of the vagina it is very important. It is where, if the woman is pregnant, the baby develops.

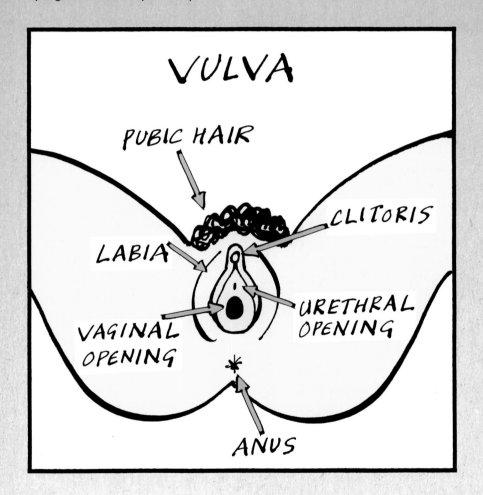

VULVA

PUBIC HAIR

CLITORIS

LABIA

VAGINAL OPENING

URETHRAL OPENING

ANUS

The genitals are the external parts of our bodies that include our sexual organs. A male's genitals are the sexual parts of his body between his legs. Visible on the outside are the:

Penis

Also known as: cock, dick, todger, prick, rod, pork sword or spam javelin. The head of the penis is the glans and the longer part is called the shaft. Inside is soft spongy tissue with lots of blood vessels. Changes in blood flow make the penis go from soft to stiff – an erection. The average size of an adult penis is 6–10cm when soft and 12–19cm when erect. The size of a man's penis does not have an effect on how good he is at sex. It's very common for a penis to curve to the left or right. Within the penis the urethra allows urine to leave the body.

Testicles/scrotum

Also known as: bollocks, balls, nuts, ball sack, gonads or plums. Beneath the penis is a bag of skin called the scrotum. Inside the scrotum two testicles hang outside the body – when fully grown these are the size of small plums – one of their slang names. The testicles produce sperm and small tubes inside the body take the semen (which contains the sperm) into the penis where they are released at ejaculation.

Getting spots and bumps on the scrotum is often completely harmless. However, as you get older you should examine your testicles when you're in the bath or shower and become familiar with the size and weight of each. Gently feel for lumps, swellings or changes in firmness. If you notice that something doesn't feel right, or you get sharp pains or a dull ache, it's important to see a doctor.

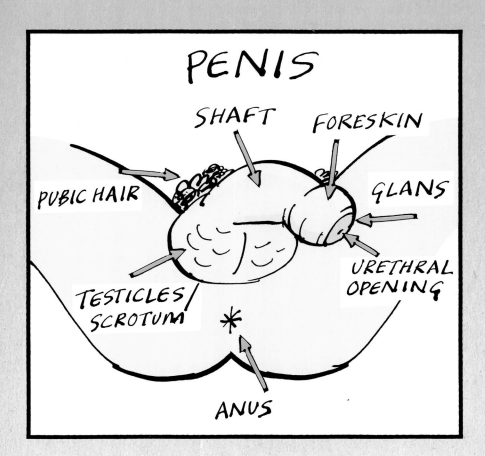

PENIS

SHAFT

FORESKIN

PUBIC HAIR

GLANS

TESTICLES/
SCROTUM

URETHRAL
OPENING

ANUS

SEE ALSO:

CIRCUMCISION page 22
DISCHARGE page 32
EJACULATION page 36
ERECTION page 38
PUBIC HAIR page 70

YOU WERE LOOKING FOR …

GONORRHOEA go to SEXUALLY
TRANSMITTED INFECTIONS
page 78
GROOMING go to INTERNET
SAFETY page 52

HIV stands for Human Immunodeficiency Virus. It is a virus that stops people's immune system from working properly. AIDS stands for Acquired Immune Deficiency Syndrome. A person with AIDS has got HIV in their immune system and can no longer fight off infections and illnesses.

HIV and AIDS are not the same thing

When somebody is described as 'living with HIV' or 'being HIV positive (+ve)' they have the HIV virus in their body. The HIV virus breaks down the immune system. When someone is described as 'having AIDS' it will be because they have a number of infections and illnesses attacking them as their immune system isn't working properly. Not everybody who is HIV+ve will get ill. People who are HIV+ve don't necessarily go on to get AIDS.

If a person is HIV+ve the virus may be transmitted through sexual contact, which makes it an STI (Sexually Transmitted Infection). However, as well as semen, vaginal and cervical secretions, HIV can also be found in blood, amniotic fluid (an essential fluid for the development of the baby within the womb) and breast milk.

Common ways of spreading HIV

- Sexual activity between two people of any gender that enables semen, vaginal fluids or blood to go from one person's body into another.
- Needles, syringes and other equipment used to inject when someone who is infected has already used them.
- From an infected mother to her baby during vaginal birth and when breastfeeding. Precautions can be taken to reduce this from happening.

Safe sex

You cannot tell if a person is HIV+ve just be looking at them. If you or they are unsure, it is essential to use condoms if you make the decision to have a sexual relationship. Condoms are the only barrier method that can stop HIV transmission in sexual relationships.

SEE ALSO:

CONDOMS page 25
CONTRACEPTION page 28
SEXUALLY TRANSMITTED
INFECTIONS page 78

YOU WERE LOOKING FOR …

HARD-ON go to ERECTION
page 38
HERPES got to SEXUALLY
TRANSMITTED INFECTIONS
page 78

The Human Papilloma Virus (HPV) is a common virus that is passed from one person to another through direct skin-to-skin contact during sexual activity. Most sexually active people will get HPV at some time in their lives, though most will never even know it.

There are about 40 types of HPV that can infect the genital areas of men and women. Most HPV types cause no symptoms and go away on their own. But it can cause genital warts and some types can cause cervical cancer in women and other less common cancers.

National HPV programme

In the UK there is a national programme to vaccinate girls aged 12 to 13 (usually in Year 8) by giving them an injection against HPV. As many as one in ten girls under the age of 16 may become infected with HPV. In order to protect as many girls as possible, the government decided to make the HPV vaccine part of schools' immunisation programmes.

A letter about the vaccine and a consent form is sent to parents before a girl has the vaccine. It is up to her whether she has the vaccine and she will want to talk this through with her parents.

Vaccines are a way to protect the body against certain diseases. They stimulate the body's natural defence mechanism, the immune system, to generate a response called antibodies, which will protect against infectious diseases.

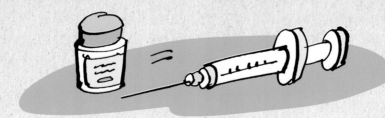

SEE ALSO:

SEXUALLY TRANSMITTED INFECTIONS page 78

YOU WERE LOOKING FOR ...

HOMOPHOBIA go to BULLYING page 19

HOMOSEXUAL go to GAY/LESBIAN page 45 and SEXUAL ORIENTATION page 77
HORMONES go to PUBERTY: BOYS page 68 and PUBERTY: GIRLS page 69

On the web there are some people with bad intentions who want to scare or harm you. Internet safety is the means you use to protect yourself online. Two main risks that people may face online are grooming and cyberbullying.

Groomers are those who trick you into believing things about them that aren't true. They may encourage you to post inappropriate information or photos. They may encourage you to meet them and tell you to keep it a secret. Cyberbullies act like real-life bullies – harming your feelings, perhaps spreading rumours or untruths about you to others online.

Ways to keep safe
- Don't post information that enables a stranger to locate you; don't use your last name, school name, sports teams, where you socialise etc.
- Protect personal information by using a 'friends' list and allow only people you know and trust to communicate with you. If you don't use privacy features, anyone can see your information.
- Avoid posting photos that allow people to identify you (for example, when they're searching for your school). Before uploading any photo, think about how you'd feel if it were seen by a parent, teacher etc. Some Internet contacts encourage 'sexting' – sending sexual messages or photos – but what happens to these after you send them?
- Be honest about your age. Membership rules are there to protect people. Most social networks expect users to be at least 13. Talk with your parents or trusted adults about joining a social network.
- Don't meet with strangers you've only communicated with online.
- Block offensive people from commenting about you.

Jealousy is something that's a natural, but rather unpleasant, part of human relationships. Jealous feelings are often angry, resentful, unkind and fault-finding. They can be harmful and damaging to relationships. Our feelings of jealousy usually occur because we feel unsure of ourselves.

There are many different types of jealousy:

- Competition between family members (especially brothers and sisters) can affect all ages and different members of any family. It's often caused because one person thinks another is getting more attention or material things than themselves.

- Jealousy in friendships often happens because someone is worried about being replaced by another person in a friendship and then being left out.

- At work, situations of jealousy can happen between people in similar job positions. Sometimes one person will receive more praise from the boss than the other; or one will get an increase in wages and the other won't.

- Where romance is involved jealousy happens perhaps because one partner feels the other partner seems to be more interested in someone else, or maybe wants to have more time to see other people.

Can you solve it?

You could start by asking yourself 'What do I feel unsure about? Do I feel unattractive? Am I worried about how the other person feels about me?' If you can, work out what it is that's really 'getting to you'. It may help to chat to a trusted friend or adult about your feelings.

KISSING

Kissing is when one person decides to use their lips to make contact with someone else. There are many different kinds of kissing and many reasons for it. Also known as: snogging or tonsil tennis.

Family kisses are usually those between parents, brothers and sisters, aunties, uncles, cousins… you know the sort of thing. Those kisses are okay as long as there are no prickly beards, moustaches or bad breath!

Next are those respectful kisses. The 'Give Mrs XXX a kiss and thank her for the present' type. These are often the sort of kisses you could live without. Possible solutions are to put out your arm and firmly shake hands with them, or if you can't get away with that, turn your face sideways and present them with your cheek.

Friends who like, respect and/or admire each other sometimes kiss. It's often given in greeting and is sometimes accompanied by a hug.

Romantic kisses are reserved for people you feel extra specially involved with. They are usually soft and gentle. Passionate kisses mostly take place when you feel really crazily in love with someone. People may use their tongues (French-kissing) so that they can feel really close to their partner.

Don't worry about learning how to kiss – it will happen naturally when it's meant to. It also gets better with practice. Remember, if you don't want to kiss someone, you don't have to.

SEE ALSO:

COLD SORES page 23
FOREPLAY page 43
PLEASURE page 64

 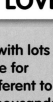

'Love' is a word with lots of meanings: love for your family is different to romantic love. Thousands of love songs and poems try to say what love is like. Songs often describe it as really wanting to be with someone, share things with them and make them happy.

Unrequited love

It can be amazing when you find out that the person you love feels the same about you. It can be very hard for us when another person doesn't seem to love us back. It can seem like the end of the world – but everyone gets over that feeling and goes on to see that it was one-sided and it wasn't going to be a happy or successful time for either person.

Love and sex

When it comes to sexual relationships, it's important not to use love to bribe someone or try to make them do things they don't want to do. 'If you really loved me, then you would…' If you do genuinely love someone then you won't want to pressure them.

One final thought. Some people who fall in love end up neglecting their friends so they can spend all their time with their boy/girlfriend. That's not a good idea – we all need friends – it doesn't have to be a choice between them and the one you love.

SEE ALSO:

CHATTING UP page 21
CRUSH page 29
DUMPING page 34
FANCYING page 41
SEX page 75

YOU WERE LOOKING FOR …

LABIA go to GENITALS: FEMALE page 46
LESBIAN go to GAY/LESBIAN page 46 and SEXUAL ORIENTATION page 77
LOVE GLOVES go to CONDOMS page 25
LUBE go to FOREPLAY page 43

MASTURBATION

Masturbation is when a person touches their genitals because it feels nice and gives them pleasure. Most people do this on their own and sometimes they do it with their sexual partner – this is called 'mutual masturbation'.

Masturbation is a very natural thing to do. Masturbation is a private thing – finding a place where you won't be disturbed is important – nobody wants to be embarrassed. Whether you masturbate or how you do it is personal to you. There is no right or wrong way.

Boys and men

A penis is very sensitive to touch. Boys and men usually masturbate by gripping the base of the penis and moving their hand up and down. Terms for male masturbation include: wanking, jerking off, tossing off, bashing the bishop, slapping the salami or spanking the monkey.

Girls and women

A girl's genitals, especially the clitoris, are sensitive to touch. Girls and women usually masturbate by stimulating their clitoris using their fingers to stroke/rub it. She will work out the best ways to do this. Terms for female masturbation include: wanking, flicking the bean or polishing the pearl.

Religion and culture

Different religions and cultures have different attitudes to masturbation. There are lots of myths e.g. it makes you go blind, it stunts your growth. None of these are true. Masturbation is not bad for you and you can do it as much, or as little, as you like. It's a natural and normal thing to do.

SEE ALSO:

ORGASM page 59
PLEASURE page 64
PORNOGRAPHY page 65

MENSTRUATION go to PERIODS page 62
MINGE go to GENITALS: FEMALE page 46
MORNING AFTER PILL go to CONTRACEPTION page 28
MUFF go to GENITALS: FEMALE page 46

YOU WERE LOOKING FOR ...

MELONS go to BREASTS page 18

Nutrition is the process of receiving important nutrients from food and drink that help keep us well. Eating well is an essential part of staying well mentally and physically.

This isn't easy as modern lifestyles mean we often eat on the run e.g. we rarely sit down to proper meals and 'graze' by snacking here and there. Teenagers need a healthy eating style to help them deal with the rapid growth that comes with adolescence.

As you begin to develop independence from your parents and spend more time with friends, eating healthily isn't always top of the agenda.

Balance, balance, balance

All food surveys show that teenagers' average consumption of saturated fat, sugar and salt is too high, while that of starchy carbohydrates and fibre is low. Try to have a healthy balance in what you eat and drink. You are going to get most of your energy from foods like bread, cereal and potatoes. Your vitamins and minerals will come from fresh fruit and vegetables and they'll help to protect your immune system, keeping you well.

A moderate amount of protein is needed for muscle development and you'll get this from meat, fish, beans etc. In order to keep teeth and bones healthy you need dairy foods. Although you don't need lots, you should have some foods with fats and sugars. If you choose to become a veggie or vegan you will stop eating some or all foods from animals so you'll need to make sure you are eating plenty of beans, pulses, nuts and other protein and iron-rich food.

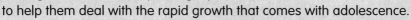

SEE ALSO:	YOU WERE LOOKING FOR ...
EATING DISORDERS page 35 FITNESS page 42	

ORAL SEX

Oral sex involves kissing, licking, sucking and sometimes gently nibbling another person's genitals. Also known as: going down on, giving a blow job, giving head, sucking off, pearl diving, cunnilingus or fellatio.

Now you might read this and think, 'Why on earth would somebody want to do that to another person?' Well, some people think it's fabulous and others think it's awful.

What does it include?
With mouth to penis sex it usually involves one person wrapping their lips around the penis and sliding their mouth up and down so that the penis slides in and out. With mouth to vulva sex one partner will gently kiss, lick and suck around the whole area.

People worry that oral sex may smell or taste bad: if you're both healthy it won't. Generally speaking vaginal and seminal fluids only smell or taste bad if they're infected. Also, your genitals won't smell if you wash them regularly – just remember never put soap into your vagina!

Oral sex is a really close, private thing for couples to do with/for each other. It is incredibly personal and should be cherished. The choice is absolutely up to those involved. As with everything to do with sex it is a matter of personal preference and no one should ever feel they have to be drawn into it if they don't want to.

SEE ALSO:
COLD SORES page 23
GENITALS: FEMALE page 46
GENITALS: MALE page 48
SEX page 75

YOU WERE LOOKING FOR ...
ODOUR go to BO page 14

Orgasm is the word usually used to indicate the intense and overwhelming excitement felt during sex. Also known as: cumming, cum, the big O, make it or pop one's cork.

Orgasms are different for males and females. With males an orgasm usually means ejaculating (cumming); this is a physical sensation and may be accompanied by emotional feelings too. With females an orgasm doesn't usually end up with a physical ejaculation of fluid, though it might. It's rare for a female to achieve orgasm through sexual intercourse on its own: most females will need to have some form of physical stimulation to the clitoris in order to reach an orgasm.

It's like…

Describing an orgasm isn't easy because every individual will experience different feelings if they have one. For some it will feel like internal muscle spasms (they don't hurt) that take over the inside of the body; for others it will feel like a rush of waves that pulse through the body.

Some people make noises when they reach orgasm and some people stay silent. The sensations of an orgasm can make people laugh or cry; make you wide-awake or sleepy. There's no right or wrong way to be. It's also worth remembering that you don't have to have an orgasm to enjoy sex!

SEE ALSO:

EJACULATION page 36
MASTURBATION page 56
PLEASURE page 64
SEX page 75

YOU WERE LOOKING FOR …

OVEREATING go to EATING
DISORDERS page 35

PMS (PRE-MENSTRUAL SYNDROME) / **PMT** (PRE-MENSTRUAL TENSION)

Some girls/women can feel strange during the time leading up to their period. This is usually due to something known nowadays as PMS and we know that around 90% of women get it.

PMS happens before the period is due and can last from two days to two weeks. The symptoms vary and can include:
• anger • anxiety • clumsiness • constipation • cravings for certain foods • feeling bloated • headaches • irritability • mood swings • putting on weight • spots • stress • tearfulness.

If you do suffer from PMS it's really worth making a note of how and when it affects you. When you work this out you can try to help yourself by altering your lifestyle a bit.

- Avoid smoking, alcohol, tea, coffee and fizzy drinks that contain caffeine: they all make PMS worse.
- Eat more foods that contain Vitamin B6 e.g. potatoes, bananas, beans, seeds, nuts, red meat, poultry, fish, eggs, spinach and fortified cereals.
- Eat small meals every three hours – this will help lighten those cravings for sweet things.
- Exercise helps too.

If your PMS is really awful and you can't cope with it then make an appointment to see your doctor – you don't have to suffer.

Just remember, when your period is over (or when it starts for some women) you'll feel back to normal again!

SEE ALSO:

DEPRESSION page 31
PERIODS page 62
PUBERTY: GIRLS page 69

How much is a person influenced by the people around them? When someone feels that they are being heavily influenced to act or speak in a certain way by their friends and others their age, we call this experience 'peer pressure'.

Sometimes peer pressure can be direct: 'act and think like me or we aren't friends; do what we do or you're not part of our crowd'. An extreme example of this can be when someone feels their only choice is to join a gang – sometimes with negative consequences.

Other pressure isn't so obvious. This can include pressure from the media, such as advertising, music and television. They can act as a gentle way to influence what you buy and what you do. If we accept these messages without thinking about them then that too is a kind of peer pressure.

Making decisions

Most people enjoy some level of joining in with others – there is nothing wrong with that. However, being able to make your own decisions and behave in a way that you feel is right and responsible is an important part of maturing and becoming an independent person. You might want to find different ways of thinking through an issue – make a point of finding out information to help you make up your own mind.

Don't forget: peer pressure is usually meant in a negative way, but our friends and peers can influence us in positive ways too – you decide.

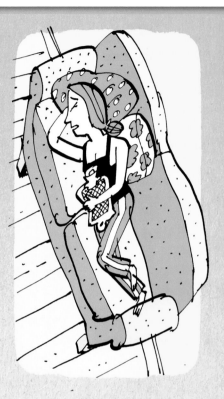

A period is a regular occurrence when a girl or a woman loses blood out through her vagina. It usually happens to women/girls about once a month, every month. Periods happen because the lining of the uterus (womb) builds up each month and if it isn't used to house a fertilised egg it comes away in the form of blood. Periods stopping are usually the first sign that a woman is pregnant (if she's involved in a sexual relationship).

Periods are also known as: menstruation, on the blob, monthlies, on the rag, being on, the curse or having the painters and decorators in.

Going through puberty takes a while and periods can start at any age: some girls start when they're eight years old and others at 15. Don't be too concerned about timings when your periods begin. You may have one period and then not have another for a few months. It usually takes quite a while for them to become regular. Periods can be affected by stress, illness, excessive weight loss and worry.

A period can last from three to seven days. It may start slowly, get heavier and ease off at the end. Periods may be painful and give you tummy cramps. If you're worried see your doctor. A female member of your family or school nurse should be able to give you some practical help and advice.

SEE ALSO:	YOU WERE LOOKING FOR ...
PMS/PMT page 60 PREGNANCY page 66 PUBERTY: GIRLS page 69 SANITARY PROTECTION page 73	PERFECTION go to BODY IMAGE page 15

Piercing and tattooing the human body have been happening for centuries. In different times and places they have been seen as attractive, ugly, sophisticated or crude. Piercing uses a spring-loaded 'gun' or needles to put holes into body parts including ears and noses to insert jewellery. Tattooing uses an electric needle to inject coloured pigment into small deep holes made in the skin to make marks or designs.

Piercing

Piercers are required to check for allergies or health problems and should give you a run-through of the whole process. They must ensure you have all the aftercare advice you need to keep the area free of infection.

The NHS estimates that 25% of people who have a piercing have complications including swelling, infections and bleeding – so finding a reputable, licensed piercer is essential. Some local councils keep registers of approved piercers who have passed hygiene and safety standards and who are regularly inspected by health and safety officers. If your parent or carer does agree to you having an ear piercing then the NHS provides a safety checklist (see *Useful contacts*).

In the UK, genital piercings on a female/male (and female nipple piercings) under the age of 16 are illegal.

Tattooing

The Tattooing of Minors Act makes it illegal for anyone to tattoo you if you are under the age of 18 – new guidelines suggest that a tattoo artist should ask to see proof of age and record this before agreeing to tattoo you.

SEE ALSO:	YOU WERE LOOKING FOR ...
BODY IMAGE page 15	PHYSICAL ABUSE go to ABUSE page 10 PILL go to CONTRACEPTION page 28 PIMPLES go to ZITS page 87

Pleasure is a natural part of sexual feelings and the reason most people enjoy sexual relationships. Sometimes some adults get worried that if young people see sex as pleasurable then this might encourage them to have an irresponsible attitude to sex.

When you *are* eventually ready for a sexual relationship then you need to think about it in terms of not just the pleasurable, physical things you might want to do but also ask yourself:

- Why you might want to take a relationship a step further – is it because you really feel you want that or because it feels as if everyone else is doing this and you're not?
- Are you and the other person making a free choice about what you do or don't want to do?
- Have you and the other person both discussed and agreed what comes next in your relationship?
- Do you both feel the same way about each other?

While pleasure is really important to a good relationship, it is not the only thing to think about when it comes to sex. One of the best ways of dealing with sex and pleasure is to talk openly and honestly about it with people we trust and who care about us. At the right time, in the right relationship, with the right person, sex can and should be really pleasurable.

SEE ALSO:

ABSTAIN page 9
AGE OF CONSENT page 12
FOREPLAY page 43
MASTURBATION page 56
SEX page 75

YOU WERE LOOKING FOR ...

PLUMS go to GENITALS: MALE page 48

Pornography ('porn') describes material in print, on the Internet, in films etc. that is sexual entertainment for adults. Pornography has been around for almost all of human existence and nowadays it is much more accessible to a wider audience because of modern technology.

Sex education?

Pornography should not be treated as a reliable source of sex education. Most pornography isn't real – the people you see in many magazines and on the Internet aren't representations of real life – they are part of people's fantasies. Most of them are chosen for how their body looks and works. Pornography can provide unrealistic views about everyday sexual relationships.

In the same way that films we see at the cinema take us into unreal worlds, such as Hogwarts School, so pornography isn't always real either.

Pornography may make sex look like it's all about doing something to someone else or having power over someone else – but in the real world sex is more complicated than that and involves sharing affections, feelings and emotions.

A negative effect

Because pornography is intended for viewing only by adults you have to be 18 or older to watch it legally. Of course younger people can access it on the Internet but research shows that it can have a negative effect and after seeing pornography some people have unrealistic ideas about themselves, relationships and sex.

SEE ALSO:

PREGNANCY

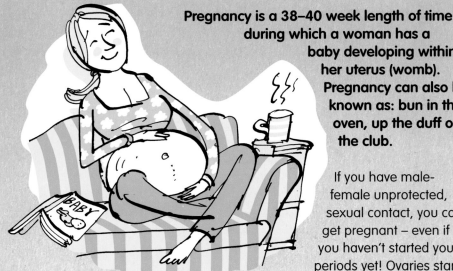

Pregnancy is a 38–40 week length of time during which a woman has a baby developing within her uterus (womb). Pregnancy can also be known as: bun in the oven, up the duff or in the club.

If you have male-female unprotected, sexual contact, you can get pregnant – even if you haven't started your periods yet! Ovaries start producing (monthly) eggs before periods start. If one of these eggs is fertilised by sperm from your partner you will become pregnant.

How can I tell if I'm pregnant?

A woman sometimes knows she is pregnant through various tell-tale signs, though not everyone has the same signs, and some people have none at all. However, generally these signs are:
- missed period or short and very light period at the usual time you would expect to have one • nipples get darker • puffy, sensitive breasts
- sickness • tiredness • vaginal discharge increases.

If a young woman thinks she might be pregnant and if she has symptoms from the list above she might feel very scared, worried or not want to believe it. However frightened she feels, she shouldn't keep this secret. Seeking help and advice straight away is the best course of action. The most sensible thing would be for her to tell her mother or another female relative. If she feels she can't do that then she should go to a doctor or young people's sexual health clinic and ask them for a pregnancy test or buy one from a pharmacy.

Choices

If she is pregnant, the next thing she needs to do is to carefully consider her choices. This again is a sensible time to involve her mother (or other female relative) and the baby's father.

There will be a lot to think about – including her education. No girl should have to leave school or have her education stopped if she is pregnant (Brook is a good agency to consult about this – see *Useful contacts*). A lot of people will probably offer suggestions on what to do. She may feel press-ganged into making a decision that might not feel right for her. If it all feels a bit too much she could visit a local counselling service or speak to a trusted adult outside the family. Everyone has their own ideas and dreams about how they want their life and future to be – so, the final decision should be hers.

The stages of pregnancy

- The human life cycle begins at fertilisation, when an egg cell inside a woman and a sperm cell from a man fuse into a single cell.
- Over the next few days, the single cell divides many times to form a hollow ball of smaller cells.
- On the sixth day after fertilisation, the hollow ball burrows into the wall of the woman's uterus (womb).
- Gradually, the cells begin to become different from one another, forming for example, the nervous system and the circulatory system.
- The first brain activity does not begin for five more months.
- One more month later, all the major organs will have formed in miniature, including ears, eyes, liver and kidneys – though they won't be working properly yet.
- At birth, the muscles of the mother's uterus begin to contract and push the baby out through the vagina. This process is called 'labour' because it is hard work and can take a long time.

SEE ALSO:

ABORTION page 8
CONTRACEPTION page 28
PERIODS page 62
SEX page 75

PUBERTY: BOYS

Puberty is a process that changes us both physically and emotionally as our bodies sexually mature. It doesn't happen suddenly – it can take months or years for all the changes to happen. During and after the puberty process, a human body is ready to reproduce – even though we may not want to (or feel ready to) have sex or start a relationship.

Physical changes

Puberty happens at different times for different people – boys can start puberty anywhere between nine or 15. Here's a list of the physical changes a boy will experience (they don't happen in any particular order):

- Body starts to grow faster and to change shape e.g. shoulders grow wider;
- Penis and testicles get bigger and start to produce sperm and can ejaculate semen;
- Hair grows on the face, under the arms, around the genitals and sometimes on other parts of the body;
- You may sweat more or develop spots on your face and body;
- The voice changes and gets deeper.

Emotional changes

The hormones that make all the physical changes happen also affect our feelings. Emotional changes include sexual feelings for other people and more mood changes – sometimes unpredictably. Puberty can leave us feeling awkward about ourselves; our bodies and emotions often seem to be outside our control.

SEE ALSO:

EJACULATION page 36
PUBIC HAIR page 70
WET DREAMS page 85
ZITS page 87

Puberty is a process that changes us both physically and emotionally as our bodies sexually mature. It doesn't happen suddenly – it can take months or years for all the changes to happen. During and after the puberty process, a human body is ready to reproduce – even though we may not want to (or feel ready to) have sex or start a relationship.

Physical changes

Not every girl goes through puberty at the same age: some girls start seeing the physical signs of puberty by the time they are eight and for others it may not happen until 15 or 16. Don't worry – we are all different. The changes that occur are:

- Hips will become wider and breasts rounder;
- Underarm and pubic hair will develop;
- External sex organs will become a bit larger and more sensitive. Periods will begin;
- Face will change too and you will probably look more grown-up;
- You may sweat more and may develop spots on your face and body.

Emotional changes

These physical changes are caused by chemicals and hormones in your body. These hormones can also affect how you feel emotionally: one minute you can feel really happy and the next angry and fed-up. It is confusing and you may think no one understands you – particularly your parents. You'll get days when you don't think any of your clothes suit you or when your hair won't go right and when you feel like crawling under a stone. Just remember you really aren't alone: your friends will have similar feelings too.

SEE ALSO:

BREASTS page 18
PMS/PMT page 60
PERIODS page 62
PUBIC HAIR page 70
ZITS page 87

P ▶ PUBIC HAIR

One of the most noticeable changes a young person experiences at puberty is the growth of hair around their genitals (also known as pubes) and armpits.

Before puberty, the genital area of both boys and girls can have very fine hair, but as puberty begins hormones known as androgens produce thicker and rougher, often curlier, hair with a faster growth rate.

Boys often notice a few sparse hairs on the scrotum or at the upper base of the penis and then within a few years thicker hair fills the pubic area. As they grow older it may spread on to the thighs and upwards on the abdomen towards the belly button. Girls usually have a more triangular pubic patch with a similar growth rate and after a few years it may spread in a similar pattern to boys.

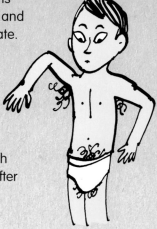

Variety

Pubic hair (and sometimes armpit hair) can vary in colour from the hair on a person's scalp. The general rule about puberty is that it can vary a lot from one person to another. Just as humans have a wide variety of head hair so pubic hair varies from tightly curled to entirely straight. Pubic hair patterns can also vary by race and ethnicity.

Pubic hair will make your genital area sweat more, so (as with armpit hair) it's important to wash regularly to keep the area clean and reduce body odours.

Rape, sometimes also called sexual assault, is forced and unwanted sexual penetration. A person who has been raped did not give their consent. It can happen to both men and women of any age. Rape is a crime, whether the person committing it is a stranger or someone you know or a family member.

If you, or someone you know, has been raped you should report the crime immediately. This may feel almost impossible if the rapist is older, a family member or someone you know. Don't worry – there are people who are specially trained who know how best to offer care and support through this.

If you have been raped

Here are three important things to do:

- Tell someone, don't keep silent. Sometimes people who are raped feel they are to blame but whatever happened wasn't their fault. No one has the right to have sex with anyone against their will. If someone says 'no' it always means no.
- Seek medical care. Even though it may feel uncomfortable, a person should get medical attention right away without changing their clothes or washing.
- Deal with the feelings that rape can leave. Someone who has been raped might feel a lot of things: anger, fear or confusion. It's also normal for someone who has been raped to feel shame or embarrassment. There are many support services that can help you. They understand how difficult it is for people to come forward and will respect and believe you.

Rape and sexual assault are violent crimes that can have a devastating effect. If this has happened to you, find someone you trust to talk to. You should tell the police or someone you know – but if you truly feel you can't, or you need help in doing so, then call ChildLine on 0800 1111.

SEE ALSO:

ABUSE page 10
AGE OF CONSENT page 12
SEXUAL HARASSMENT page 76

YOU WERE LOOKING FOR …

RACISM go to BULLYING page 19

When we hear the word 'relationships' our first thoughts are probably about those that are romantic and close on a one-to-one basis. Those relationships can be very special, but may not happen for all of us.

Types of relationship

We will all have a number of different types of relationships throughout our lives, such as:

- Family relationships – sometimes smooth and happy and at other times bumpy and annoying;
- Friendships between two or more people that provide companionship and come about through familiarity and shared interests;
- Those between ourselves and a person who offers us their services e.g. hairdresser, newsagent;
- Those which involve confidentiality in order for us to gain help e.g. with a pharmacist, our doctor or other medical professionals;
- Romantic relationships, where you are very close to your partner, may hold hands, kiss and cuddle and buy special gifts for each other;
- Sexual relationships, involving all types of sexual intimacy, not just intercourse, but also oral sex, mutual masturbation etc.

Qualities for a good relationship

For all relationships, there are some qualities which will make them work better for the people involved.

- Communication – listening and clearly expressing yourself.
- Honesty – speaking openly about your relationship.
- Balance – reserve time for other friends and activities outside 'the relationship'. The relationship can wear out very quickly if you just rely on seeing and doing things only with that one person.

When you start having periods you will need to use sanitary protection to absorb the blood that comes out of your vagina, during the day and night.

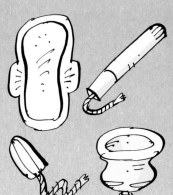

Types of sanitary protection

- 'Panty liners' are very slim and might be sufficient at the beginning and end of each period, when flow is light.
- Press-on pads or towels come in different shapes and sizes. They are soft and absorbent with plastic at the back that stops them leaking. Usually these have a strip of sticky tape on one side so that you can stick them inside your knickers. Some have side panels (wings) that fold over the edge of your knickers and keep them even more firmly in place.
- Tampons are made of tightly rolled cotton with a string at one end. They are pushed inside the vagina and as they absorb the blood they expand. Some tampons come with smooth cardboard tube applicators; others are designed to be inserted just using your fingers.
- Menstrual cups or moon cups are worn inside the vagina to collect blood. They are cheaper and more environmentally-friendly than towels, pads and tampons. However, you may find them messier to use.

You will need to change your sanitary protection regularly – at least every four hours. It's easier to judge this if you start by using towels or pads. It is always best to discuss the options with your mother or another female relative – as she will have experienced periods too.

Toxic Shock Syndrome (TSS) is a serious and rare illness that can happen during periods. It is caused by bacteria which can produce toxins (poisons). It has been linked to the absorbency of tampons, therefore using sanitary towels/pads instead of tampons at night is a good idea.

SELF-HARM

Self-harm is when someone deliberately injures themselves, usually by cutting, scratching or pricking to draw blood, burning, picking at old wounds, punching or head-banging a wall.

It's a hidden behaviour – we don't know exactly how many people self-harm. However, females aged 15–19 and males aged 20–24 seem to be most affected.

Why do people self-harm?

The reasons why people self-harm are complex but it isn't about attention-seeking or wanting to die. People may feel bad about themselves and negative things may have happened to them like abuse, bullying or family relationships going wrong. Pressure builds up and they feel the physical pain provides a relief to their emotions. They may feel the cutting acts like a pressure valve, allowing them to relax.

Self-harmers usually want to stop, but don't know what else to do to express their emotions. If you have those feelings of self-harm yourself then try doing something else to break the pattern. Some people find beating up a pillow, squeezing an ice cube or flicking an elastic band lets them work on their feelings. Stop being self-critical and tell someone. Everyone has times like this and it's important to know that there are other ways of dealing with it.

Helping a friend who self-harms

If you suspect a friend is self-harming, don't be critical; listen to them, encourage them to talk about their feelings and stop keeping things a secret. Do everything you can to persuade them to get professional help – but remember, it's not your fault if they do harm. Be self-aware and don't join in with them.

SEE ALSO:

DEPRESSION page 31
EMOTIONAL GOOD HEALTH page 37

YOU WERE LOOKING FOR …

SEPARATION go to DIVORCE page 33

When we hear the word 'sex' most people think of one particular sexual activity – sexual intercourse. This is when a man and a woman feel very close and attracted to each other. The closest physical contact that they can have is when the man's erect penis goes inside the woman's vagina. The vagina will stretch for the penis to fit inside it. Sex can also be known as: having it off, fucking, bonking or shagging.

There are many words and expressions used to describe sexual intercourse: one of the most common is 'making love'. Hugging, cuddling, kissing and stroking are also expressions of love but sexual intercourse is the most intimate.

Sexual intercourse isn't just about physical contact and it helps to remember the emotional and physical consequences.

- Having sex will change how you feel about the other person.
- Sex can lead to a woman becoming pregnant. It is also possible to pass on viruses and infections from one person to the other.
- Waiting until you are old enough to make the decision to have sex will help you keep safe and enjoy the experience. Everyone can decide not to have sex; it's okay to say 'no' or change your mind and say you don't want to do it again.

Two partners of the same gender (male: male, or female: female) can also enjoy having a sexual relationship. Except for the possibility of becoming pregnant, they have to think about the same issues as heterosexuals.

To harass somebody means to annoy, bother or pester them. So, sexual harassment means when someone else does this to you in a sexual way or about sexual things.

Verbal and physical

A person may make comments about your body or the way you look, they may talk about sexual things when you don't want to. They might do any of these things directly to you or shout them out when you're around or near them.

Sexual harassment can also be physical: a person may try to 'touch you up', grab you, block your way, try to kiss you, get too close physically and hassle you in a way you don't like or want.

You have the right to say 'no' to any of this, whether it's physical or not. Sexual harassment is something that can happen to you whether you're a boy or a girl and whether you're gay, straight or bisexual.

Getting help

Sexual harassment isn't a nice thing to go through and it can be hard to make your feelings about it clear to other people. If at first you're not taken seriously, talk about it to another person until you find someone who understands why you want this to stop.

Sexual harassment is a form of sexual abuse and people don't always like to talk about it. However, keeping silent does no one any good. If harassment isn't reported it might continue and other people might find they are being harassed too.

SEE ALSO:

ABUSE page 10
BULLYING page 19
RAPE page 71

YOU WERE LOOKING FOR ...

SEXTING go to INTERNET SAFETY
page 52
SEXUAL ABUSE go to ABUSE
page 10

Each person's sexuality is made up of factors such as their personal feelings, their gender and their sexual orientation. Sexual orientation means the pattern of whom we are romantically and sexually attracted to – in other words, the people we fancy.

Most people talk about three sexual orientations or patterns:
- **Heterosexual** ('straight') – meaning we feel attraction towards somebody of the opposite gender to ourselves;
- **Homosexual** ('gay' and 'lesbian') – meaning we feel attraction towards somebody of the same gender as ourselves;
- **Bisexual** ('bi') – meaning we feel attraction towards people of both our own and the opposite gender.

Sometimes people talk about a fourth sexual orientation – asexual, meaning having no romantic or sexual attraction to anyone.

Discovering your sexuality

All young people go through a process of discovering their sexual identity and determining whether they are heterosexual, lesbian, gay or bisexual. Sometimes the pattern of attraction changes over a person's lifetime – for most people it seems to remain unchanged.

Heterosexuality is the majority pattern and people who don't belong to that pattern have often had to deal with prejudice and misunderstanding. Despite past intolerance, there is nothing wrong with being lesbian, gay, bi-sexual – or even heterosexual.

There is no simple, single cause for explaining why a person has a particular sexual orientation. It's important to know that discriminating against someone because of their sexual orientation is illegal.

SEE ALSO:

These are infections which are mainly passed from one person to another during sex.

If you are having a sexual relationship of any kind, you should always use condoms. Condoms will help protect you and your partner from transmitting STIs to each other. If you have any unusual symptoms (particularly from, on or around your genitals) or unexplained illness, then don't ignore this. Go to a sexual health, young person's clinic or your GP. You will be treated in complete confidence, without any fuss and nobody will judge you.

There are many different STIs and most don't show any symptoms at all. However, if you have had sex and get any of the following symptoms you should visit a clinic:
- Painful or frequent urination;
- Sores or scaly patches on the genitals;
- Abnormal discharge from the penis or vagina;
- Anal itching, discomfort, bleeding or discharge.

The STIs that young people need to be most aware of are:

Chlamydia
Symptoms: Most people don't have any symptoms, though abdominal cramps and pain on urinating may occur
Effects: Left untreated this can cause infertility
Treatment: Antibiotics

Genital Warts
Symptoms: Small, fleshy bumps appear around the genital or anal area
Effects: Can be uncomfortable and ugly
Treatment: Ointments or freezing – done by medical professionals

Gonorrhoea
Symptoms: Most women and some men don't have any symptoms, though pain on urinating may occur. There may also be noticeable discharge from the vagina, which may be thick and green or yellow, or discharge from the tip of the penis, which may be white, yellow or green.
Effects: If untreated can cause lots of problems including infertility
Treatment: Antibiotics

Herpes
Symptoms: Small painful blisters or sores on the genitals
Effects: Painful when outbreaks of sores occur
Treatment: No cure but tablets and cream can reduce the severity

HIV/AIDS
See page 30

Pubic Lice (Crabs – not the same as head lice/nits)
Symptoms: Severe itching
Effects: No long-term health problems, but will remain if untreated
Treatment: Special lotions which can be bought in pharmacies

'Stress' means the feeling of pressure or anxiety about something. Stress can be caused by schoolwork piling up, preparing for exams, being teased or bullied or having problems at home or elsewhere.

Symptoms

Even though stress may affect you physically your body is designed to be able to cope with sudden or occasional stresses e.g. if you are in danger adrenaline pumps through your body to help you react more quickly. However, your body is less able to cope with longer-lasting stressful situations. These can make you feel tired, make you go off your food and find it difficult to sleep and can cause stomach aches or headaches.

Dealing with stress

There are ways that you can help yourself if things are getting too stressful. Different strategies will work for different people. Some people say these help:

- Go for a walk, kick a ball around, take part in a physical activity;
- Give yourself time to relax and a bit of a treat;
- Re-focus your mind on something else e.g. watching a DVD;
- Sleep or chill out.

Even when we develop our own strategies to help us deal with stress, there can be times when we feel overwhelmed by the situation and forget to use them. To get to the bottom of any stressful problem you will almost always have to talk over your feelings with somebody you trust.

SEE ALSO:
BEREAVEMENT page 13
DEPRESSION page 31
EMOTIONAL GOOD HEALTH page 37
EXAMS page 39

YOU WERE LOOKING FOR ...
STERILISATION go to CONTRACEPTION page 28
STIFFY go to ERECTION page 38
STUDY go to EXAMS page 39
SPUNK go to EJACULATION page 36
SWEAT go to BO page 14

Thrush is a common yeast-like fungus infection that can cause itching and inflammation of the genitals. Both men and women can get thrush. It is not technically a sexually transmitted infection (STI); many people can have small amounts of the fungus in their body before they have any sexual contact.

Women

Signs of thrush can be a creamy-white discharge and pain when peeing. Vaginal thrush isn't dangerous but it can be uncomfortable. The fungus that causes thrush lives on the skin, in the mouth, gut and vagina. Thrush doesn't normally cause any problems but sometimes it can grow out of control. Causes of thrush include:

- Not taking care when you go to the loo. Remember to wipe from front to back, to avoid spreading bacteria from your bottom to your vagina.
- Wearing tight clothing and underwear;
- Taking certain antibiotics;
- Using products that irritate the vagina e.g. vaginal deodorant or bubble bath.

Men

Symptoms could include:

- Itching or burning under the foreskin or at the tip of the penis;
- Sore-looking, or red patches on the penis or under the foreskin;
- A creamy-white discharge under the foreskin;
- Pain when peeing.

A doctor or sexual health clinic will know if you've got thrush by giving you a simple and painless test. It requires taking a swab which is wiped round the inside of the vagina or on the end of the penis.

SEE ALSO:

SEXUALLY TRANSMITTED INFECTIONS page 78
UNDERWEAR page 83

PROTECTION page 73
TATTOOS go to PIERCINGS/TATTOOS page 63
TERMINATION go to ABORTION page 8
TESTICLES go to GENITALS: MALE page 48

YOU WERE LOOKING FOR …

TAMPONS go to SANITARY

TITS go to BREASTS page 18

TRANSGENDER/TRANSSEXUAL

Sometimes a person feels that they were born into the wrong body. They describe themselves as having the identity of a boy but living in a girl's body, or the identity of a girl but living in a boy's body. The technical name for this is 'gender dysphoria' and a person may describe themselves as transsexual or transgendered.

Gender identity issues vary a lot from person to person. Many adults who are transsexual had those feelings from an early age, others find that their feelings change as they reach adulthood.

The Gender Identity Research and Education Society (GIRES) estimates that about one in 4,000 of the British population is receiving medical help for gender dysphoria. Boys with gender dysphoria outnumber girls by about five to one.

Dealing with being transgender

People can deal with this issue in various ways e.g. some choose to live life in the opposite gender with appropriate clothing. Others take hormones to change the way their bodies develop. A few go a step further and have physical changes made to their body – they could have surgery to become a man or a woman permanently: a 'sex change operation'.

It's important to understand that this issue is totally different from being a transvestite (where a person likes dressing up in clothes of the opposite gender but doesn't feel that they're in the wrong body). It also isn't about being gay/lesbian (where a person is sexually attracted to someone of the same gender as themselves).

SEE ALSO:

SEXUAL ORIENTATION page 77

YOU WERE LOOKING FOR ...

TODGER go to GENITALS: MALE page 48
TOXIC SHOCK SYNDROME go to SANITARY PROTECTION page 73

UNDERWEAR (IN OTHER WORDS, KEEPING CLEAN) U

As you get older your body changes – the hormones that make puberty happen are working overtime – they produce lots of good effects but they also create some problems. One of these is that your body sweats more and your glands produce more oily products. These two things together mean that warm damp places (under your arms, between your legs and even your feet) can become breeding grounds for bacteria.

It's not just washing your body regularly that will help, it's also about wearing clean underwear each day. At this time in your life and from now on, wearing the same pair of pants two days running can make you unpleasant to sit next to. And smelly trainers and socks have the same effect!

Another thing you need to know about underwear: natural fibres like cotton are best because they absorb rather than cause you to sweat. It's helpful not to wear tight underwear too.

'Going commando'

If you are ever tempted to 'go commando' i.e. not wear underpants under your clothing, remember there is a minor risk that you'll get a rash. This is because the delicate skin around your genitals can chafe easily.

SEE ALSO:	YOU WERE LOOKING FOR ...
BO page 14	UNCIRCUMCISED go to
BRA page 17	CIRCUMCISION page 22
THRUSH page 81	VAGINA go to GENITALS: FEMALE page 46
	VAGINAL RING go to CONTRACEPTION page 28

Being a 'virgin' is a way of describing someone who hasn't had sexual intercourse. People talk about 'losing my virginity' when they had sexual intercourse for the first time. The average age of first intercourse is 16 in the UK – but that's an average age, not the age that is necessarily right for you.

If you are under the age of 16 you haven't reached the legal 'age of consent' when you can agree to sex. Once you are 16, make the decision to have a sexual relationship only when you feel you have met a person who you really trust. You both need to understand safer sex, contraception and the joys/complications that having a sexual relationship can bring. If you aren't sure you're ready, you're probably not, no matter how old you are or however long you've been with your boy/girlfriend.

Don't worry about what your friends are doing
You might feel inexperienced compared to your friends. You're an individual – don't let what other people say they are doing stop you from doing what's right for you.

If it helps to know what others are thinking, a BBC Advice survey of sexually active young people aged 12 to 17 reported that:
- 63% said they wished they had waited longer before becoming sexually active;
- 89% would advise their own brother, sister or friend not to have sex until at least after finishing secondary school.

 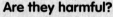

When a boy's body begins to sexually mature at puberty he starts to be able to produce sperm which is in a fluid called semen. Sometimes when he is asleep he may have an ejaculation and semen may come out of his penis. This is called 'having a wet dream'.

If you have a wet dream you might wake up and think you have wet the bed. But you haven't – urine and semen both come out of the penis but never at the same time. This first happens when puberty starts and can go on for the rest of a man's life. However, not all boys and men have wet dreams – it just depends on how your body works.

Stains

Wet dreams are nothing to be embarrassed about. They can leave a sticky mess and they are a perfectly natural part of puberty. It may seem awkward to explain stains on your sheets or clothing to anyone who does the laundry in your home – but most people will understand this is just a natural part of life. If stains are a problem, it's not a bad idea to wear shorts in bed.

Are they harmful?

There are some myths that wet dreams weaken the body or 'use up the supply of sperm'. But this is quite untrue. Wet dreams are just the body's natural response to its hormones and do not harm your health.

You need to remember that you are special and unique. Even if you're an identical twin, triplet, quad or whatever, there is only one you! You have special characteristics, talents and abilities that make you who you are.

Bad days

Sometimes we have 'off-days' when perhaps we don't feel happy, can't seem to do anything right and feel we've wrecked our chances of success. Nobody knows why this happens but it does – and it happens no matter how young or old we are. It's at times like these that we need to remember all the things we've achieved in our lives and what we are most proud of. We are still worthwhile.

Your future in your hands

Use your imagination and take yourself to the places and future you dream about. When you're there what skills will you have? What will your personal qualities be and what things will you accomplish or achieve? Daydreams are a great way to consider what we want in life – but don't just rely on dreaming. You need to appreciate that your future is in your own hands and with the right kind of planning and effort you can make your own wishes come true. Do something positive, focus on the most important goal in your life right now and plan a way to achieve it.

SEE ALSO:

CONFIDENCE page 26
EMOTIONAL GOOD HEALTH
page 37

Zits are small round swellings on the skin. Also known as: blackheads, whiteheads, acne, spots or pimples.

In puberty, the hormones that create zits on your skin are the same ones that affect your scalp and hair. The sebaceous glands in your skin produce extra oil which has the unwanted effect of making your hair greasy and your skin spotty.

The causes

The exact causes of these skin problems are unknown. A whole combination of factors means you might be more likely to have zits compared to others. These factors include the rate of puberty (it's different for different people), a family history of acne, and a person's skin type. Girls are more likely to have spots during their period. There's no definitive proof that a certain type of diet, inadequate washing, stress or any particular personal lifestyle or habit actually causes acne. Acne is something that happens to you – it's not something you've done to yourself.

What you can do

If you think you have got a problem then there are a few different acne washes and skin treatments available – try them out and see if they help. But be careful: over-washing or treating your skin might equally cause irritation.

Skin problems can make you lack confidence. If this happens to you then don't feel down. In severe cases you could go and see your doctor, who may be able to give you medication to help. For most people, though, it's a stage our bodies go through – it usually clears up in time.

SEE ALSO:

BODY IMAGE page 15
COLD SORES page 23
PUBERTY: BOYS page 68
PUBERTY: GIRLS page 69

'There is no such thing as a stupid question' – by this we mean that there will be lots of things that you will want to know more about. It is okay to ask questions to help you understand what is going on with you and your body as you are growing up, going through puberty and wanting to know more about sex.

Included here is a list of helpful agencies that can be a starting point to find out more information – they have websites and helplines that you can contact. You can also ask in libraries if there is something you want to look up and read more about.

Choosing the right person to ask questions to is also important. Lots of people find it difficult to talk about sex: some get giggly, some avoid it by saying you don't need to know, others go silent or tell you to shut-up. That's normal but not helpful.

It's best if you can start asking questions at home – it may feel awkward at first to talk to parents but in fact they know you better than anyone else. If they seem unsure about answering it's probably because they are embarrassed or find it hard to say that they don't know the answer. Take that opportunity to do some research together to find out what you want to know.

It may be easiest to ask your friends but they might not have the correct or full information. So who else would be able to help? Think about older family members who you find easy to talk to, friends' parents who you get on with, youth workers, teachers at school, and of course the school nurse.

GENERAL

If you're not sure who to talk to or where to begin to raise a problem then ChildLine is a good starting point. It's a confidential, free, 24-hour service for children and young people.
ChildLine
Telephone helpline: 0800 1111
web: **www.childline.org.uk**

ABORTION

For facts and information on abortion:
web: **http://www.efc.org.uk/young_people/facts_about_abortion.html**
For an information leaflet on abortion written for young people:
web: **www.fpa.org.uk/information**
For free and confidential information, also see Brook listed under Sexual Health/Young People's Clinics page 92.

ADOPTION

British Agencies for Adoption and Fostering offer advice, help and support e.g. tracing and contacting family members, the law and regulations.
web: **www.baaf.org.uk**

BEREAVEMENT

Grief Encounter is a project where you can get help, recognition and understanding following your loss.
Telephone: 020 8371 8455
email: contact@griefencounter.org.uk
web: **www.griefencounter.org.uk** or
web: **www.childhoodbereavementnetwork.org.uk/subIndex_youngperson.htm**

BODY IMAGE

Spoof video exposing the magic of computer trickery used in making celebrities 'beautiful': **www.youtube.com/watch?v=S_vVUIYOmJM**

CONTRACEPTION

See Sexual Health/Young People's Clinics page 92

DIVORCE/SEPARATION
The charity a kidspace is a support programme for children going through family breakdown.
web: **www.akidspace.co.uk/**

EMOTIONAL HEALTH
Get Connected is a free service that includes a 'webchat' facility for young people advising on how to get the best help.
Telephone: 0808 808 4994
web: **www.getconnected.org.uk**

NSPCC specialises in child protection and the prevention of cruelty to children.
web: **www.nspcc.org.uk**

Samaritans is a 24-hour telephone helpline.
Chris, PO Box 9090, Stirling FK8 2SA
Telephone helpline: 08457 90 90 90
email: jo@samaritans.org
web: **www.samaritans.org**

Youth Access provides information on youth counselling.
Telephone: 020 8772 9900
web: **www.youthaccess.org.uk**

YoungMinds is a national charity committed to improving the mental health of all babies, children and young people.
Telephone: 020 7089 5050
web: **www.youngminds.org.uk**

FAMILY PLANNING
Brook – See Sexual Health page 92

HEALTH

Teenage Health Freak provides information for teens on healthy eating, bullying, body changes, alcohol, drugs, accidents, moods, sex and not feeling well.
web: **www.teenagehealthfreak.org**

The BBC have a good advice website.
web: **www.bbc.co.uk/radio1/advice**

HIV/AIDS

The only way a person can find out if they have HIV/AIDS is to have a simple test at a sexual health or young people's clinic. If the test shows they are HIV+ve excellent treatment is available in the UK.

There are a number of places that you can turn to for HIV/AIDS-related help and advice. Many are listed on the Avert website.
web: **www.avert.org/aids-help-uk.htm**
The Terrence Higgins Trust (THT) also offers a range of services tailored to suit the varied needs of the diverse communities throughout the UK.
web: **www.tht.org.uk/howwecanhelpyou**
Telephone: 0808 802 1221 for an adviser

INTERNET SAFETY

www.childnet.com and **www.thinkuknow.com** are good places to find out more information.

LESBIAN, GAY, BISEXUAL

Avert is an organisation that provides information about HIV and AIDS but it also has a good general section which helps people to think more about gay or lesbian issues.
web: **www.avert.org/teens.htm**

✔ USEFUL CONTACTS

London Lesbian and Gay Switchboard provides free and confidential support and information to lesbian, gay, bisexual and transgendered communities throughout the UK.
Telephone: 0300 330 0630 (daily 10am – 11pm).

PIERCINGS
The NHS provides a safety checklist to bear in mind when visiting a piercer – you should be able to answer 'yes' to all the questions before using that piercer.
www.nhs.uk/Conditions/Body-piercing/Pages/Recommendations.aspx

PREGNANCY
Read more at **www.brook.org.uk/pregnancy/having-a-baby#school**

SEXUAL HEALTH/YOUNG PEOPLE'S CLINICS
There are excellent clinics all over the country – so there's bound to be one near you. At Brook there are no age restrictions at all (unless you count being under 25 years old), so we would advise you contact them to find your nearest clinic:
web: **www.brook.org.uk**
Telephone: 0808 802 1234 (free from all telephones including mobile phones)
Text *Ask Brook* on 07717 989 023 (standard SMS rates apply)

TRANSGENDER
Mermaids provides information and support for people who want to know more about transgender issues.
web: **www.mermaidsuk.org.uk/index.html**
See also London Lesbian and Gay Switchboard above